Erin is a poet, performer anc
performed her work all ov‹
including at the Roundhouse, t
Literature Festival, Camp Bestiv
is a former Roundhouse Resid
Festival Slam Champion, and ⸺ ⸺⸺⸺⸺⸺⸺⸺ ⸺y
the Royal Academy of Art, E4, Nationwide Building Society and
BBC Radio Stoke. Her writing and performances have been
praised for their wit and warmth.

Erin's favourite part of a cooked breakfast is the hash browns
(always plural, please), and she is happy to dip most food into
most drinks.

What We Leave Behind

Erin Bolens

Copyright © 2018 Erin Bolens

The author asserts the moral right under the Copyright, Designs and Patents Act 1988 to be identified as the author of this work.

All rights reserved. No part of this publication may be reproduced, stored in a retrieval system, or transmitted, in any form or by any means without the prior written consent of the author, nor be otherwise circulated in any form of binding or cover other than that in which it is published and without a similar condition being imposed on the subsequent purchaser.

This edition published by Bx3 an imprint of Burning Eye Books 2018

Burning Eye Books
15 West Hill, Portishead, BS20 6LG

ISBN 978-1-911570-58-5

Some people get tattoos.
I see them stroking them fondly.
I don't know how I'd draw you on me.
I don't have enough skin.
There isn't enough ink.

This is an edited version of a live show. It was first performed in full at the Roundhouse in May 2017. The conversations written as dialogue are performed half recorded, half live. All of the bold sections are accompanied by live music and can be read as one story.

Written and performed by: Erin Bolens
Director: Roberta Zuric
Music written and performed by: Sam Lunn
Film/photography and sound support: Lyall Stephens

Lyall Stephens

Steve Stephens

WHAT WE LEAVE BEHIND 13
  EPILOGUE 48

SEAMS 53
  WHEN DEAD WAS MY FAVOURITE COLOUR 55
  WHAT NOT TO BURY 56
  UPSTAIRS 57
  BILLY 58
  VEGETARIAN 59
  PHYLLIS 60
  GEORGE 61
  EDNA 62
  KEN 63
  THE TRICK 64
  LITTLE ONE 65
  FOSSILS 66
  IF YOU WERE NOT DEAD 67

What We Leave Behind

Hello. Welcome. Thank you for coming.
Sorry for the late notice.
I think it has all come together.
Today's the day.
They've hired a car for you,
blacked-out windows and everything,
as if you are a celebrity. Or a criminal.
There are flowers everywhere, the music's on standby
and there will be one hell of a buffet.
Everyone is here.
Well, most of them.
Probably the ones you'd guess.
The ones you pictured in your mind.
You did picture this, didn't you?
I do that sometimes.
Wow, there's an array of colours.
Your aunt has gone with navy;
she said you wouldn't have wanted her to buy anything especially.
Dave, Dogless Dave from round the corner,
you know, always has a lead but never a dog?
Well, Dogless Dave has bought black Crocs for the occasion
and no one has ever seen him so smart.
Janet does wear black, from head to toe actually,
but only because she has done every day since the divorce,
but no one mentions that anymore.
You look lovely, Janet. No, really. Very flattering.
Your mates all have purple socks on,
because, well, you remember Sockgate.
They all file in,
leaving their breath in the little porch with the umbrellas.
And there you are,
in the middle,
ready for the party you never planned.

For a while, there's been a lot of their stuff in the loft.
I've been putting this off.
It's time to see
if those who owned it once
left any of themselves in these things
or if they are just empty snakeskins.
Can you throw away memory?
Is that even possible?
Maybe that's why all of our attics are so full.
People kept in boxes in the loft.
Is that the right way to grieve?
Am I doing it right?

If you're not in the loft,
where do you go?
Where will you be
when your body is dust on a mantelpiece in an urn
that looks a bit like a trophy but it's not?
Or you're underground in an unnecessarily solid lacquered box
that cost more than you ever dared spend on yourself.
Or, like my dad, you are lowered down in an environmentally friendly,
ethically sourced cardboard coffin
that holds you just long enough
before you meet the worms that will show you the ropes
and the roots that will feast between your bones.
Where are you then?
After a few people throw in handfuls of soil,
before someone sensibly suggests,
This would be a lot easier with a spade.
Shall we leave it to the blokes,
go stand round the buffet?
Where are you then?
Because they'll need something.
That crowd of stoic people pretending
not to enjoy the trays of cakes too much,
they'll need something to turn to
when that something isn't you.
I've been wondering what we're leaving them,
other than unlived days,
what-ifs, might-haves, would-theys.

At the party, someone is reading a poem they say was your favourite.
No one corrected them, so it must be true.
The man at the front gives everyone a guided tour of your life
even though they know it already
and he never actually met you.

Tissues become currency, guards fall
and everyone knows
they won't be able to remember what happened
once they leave this room,
not really.

Your face is everywhere.
They used that picture.
You knew they would.
The awful one.
It grins up from every seat.
Some hold it close,
others turn it over.
Sorry, no, it is a nice... I just.

Such a lovely picture.
Yeah.
Have you put it up anywhere?
Um, no, not yet, not that one.
Be nice to frame it, maybe, wouldn't it?
Yeah, maybe.
That'd look lovely in your lounge, that one, don't you think?
Maybe, yeah.
So nice.
Yeah.
Have you got a nice frame?
Yeah, somewhere.
I could bring one round.
I think I've got one—
I'll bring one round.
OK.
No, no trouble.
Right. Thank you.

My mum holds her mum
in a handful of photographs,
a Singer sewing machine
a silk headscarf.
A woman I've met only in my mind.
She was a dot-to-dot I filled in as a child
and shaded in ever since,
adding colour occasionally
in new hues of empathy
I collect with age and mistakes.
My mum holds the best pencils in her memories.
I know I should ask her to shade with me
before the lead snaps.
We're all doing so much living, though, aren't we?
Sometimes there's no time for that.
So one day
everything she's become,
every thing she left behind
will become my brother's and mine.
Someone gone, way before our time.

I have more to hold my dad in.
Things he gave me, things I gave him,
almost enough photographs,
lists he wrote,
a guitar that sits in my brother's room like a baton,
not intentionally passed on,
clothes that dazzle you
like a rainbow spilt on them.
My mum and I made quilts of them –
this one is patches of clothes I outgrew
and ones that outlived him.
Over the years I have stitched guilt into the hem
because of how embarrassed they made me
when they were used for purpose –
I mean, literally, most of this would be at home in the circus –
but somehow now
the mismatched work of this stitched patchwork
wraps me up in glad.
A different quilt made from different clothes
would have meant a different dad.
I'd have been a different daughter.

I try, on the coldest nights, to learn to let that make me warmer.

Peter Hose

Soon, your family are thanking people
they hardly know for coming
with a sincerity that surprises them too.
They look around the hall,
still hoping to see you.
Where are you then?
Where will they look first?
Maybe they'll find you in the songs they've just heard.

Do you know what tune will represent you?
What funeral mood will it set?
Joy, regret?
I have no idea what I'd play at mine –
I didn't think I'd really mind
until I looked up what most people use.
Bearing in mind there are 26 million songs on iTunes you could choose,
as of a Co-op survey in 2014 the most played songs at British funerals were as follows:

1. 'Always Look on the Bright Side of Life'. (A littlemacabre, perhaps, but fine.)

2. 'The Lord Is My Shepherd'. (A classic – makes me think of Dawn French. Everyone loves Dawn French.)

3. 'Abide with Me'. (Not my choice, but in some rooms – not a dry eye in the house. Fine.)

4. *Match of the Day* theme tune. (The fourth. Just read that list again and take a moment to think about it.)

Moral of the story? Make sure anyone and everyone you know is aware of what you would like played at your funeral. If they don't know, there is a statistically high chance they will choose the theme tune of a football highlights show.
'Ave a word.

People squeeze your brother's shoulder a lot,
then question why they felt they had right to do that.
He doesn't mind; he can hardly see them.

Your mum doesn't know if she wants to run away
or stay in this hall forever.
At least you are still the centre point here,
your name is not an imposter yet,
she leans on it, crutch-like, in every conversation.

Others have sewn their feelings in buttonholes,
their grief becomes a bracelet
that goes with every outfit.
Hanging heavy at first,
it blends into the wrist,
they can keep it on to shower,
somehow it never rusts
and it bleeps to remind them of those that they miss.

Nips the skin as memories fade
and it becomes harder to imagine your reflections
or guess at your interjections.
If they ever took it off there would be
a pale ring around their lives
that the sun hasn't touched.

When my grief bleeps I go looking for him in things.
To see if they can help me recognise him
through these older eyes.
That's hard sometimes.

It looked the same for a while –
our life, their room, his side of the bed.
Slowly things find themselves in boxes somehow.

Under the bed becomes a museum
you wish never got planning permission,
but occasionally I would buy myself a ticket.
Hold his life in a box and then start to unpick it.

On one of those bedside trips I found this

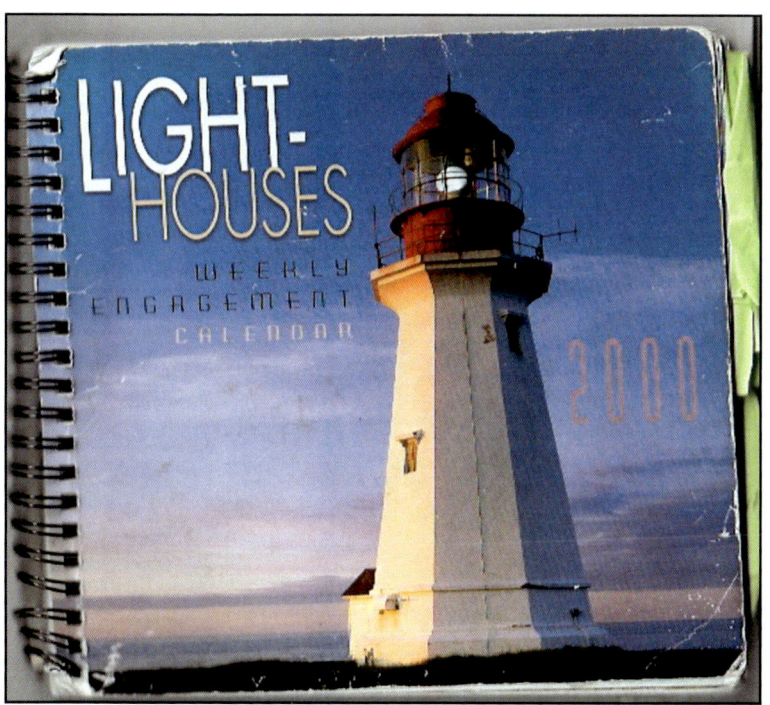

amongst the ping-pong bats and outrageous hats.

There's something so exciting about reading someone's writing.
When I found it I grasped it like the hand of a child in a busy street,
a hold that says, You stay with me,
and I dived in.

6th Feb: Go to allotment
14th Feb is marked with a heart in biro
March 12th: Don't forget salmon sausages (underlined twice)
May 1st: Danced around the maypole
May 2nd: Bees swarming
May 21st: Saw a baby shrew
Edna's birthday
Lyall's birthday
Sara's birthday
Paul's birthday

It bubbles warm in me,
knowing I will have to wait to the end to see
my December the first birth marked like that,
like anticipating the end of a book you've already read.
My heart beats fast.

June 5th: Feeling perky but tired from driving
June 10th: Rebecca's party – good party xxxxx
Glastonbury Festival is marked with arrows down all the days.
    I do that.
August 20th: (Steve's Birthday) – his birthday, marked modestly in brackets.
September 12th: Keep practising flamenco pieces
October 25th: Read kitchen gardens
November 27th: Dad phoning 10pm
December the 1st…

…is blank.
It's not there.
I turn,
check the date,
numbers not my forte,
but I thought I knew my birthday.
It's not marked.
It's okay.
Not a sign.

All fine.
Obviously.
It's obvious he
forgot innocently.
I know it holds no meaning
but you still get this feeling.

As doubt begins to give me a shoulder massage
it all crumbles down.
Tumbles out.
I'm crying on my dad's side of the bed,
insecurities written in invisible ink on the first of December 2000.
Telling myself it's not a sign.

Maybe he's not here after all.
I mean, lighthouses, for example, hold absolutely no significance.
You were probably thinking he was a massive a lighthouse fan,
with all the lighthouse paraphernalia, and why not?

Because this is all you've got to know of him
and in this minute it's all I've got to show of him.
It's just dates.

I decide it's not what I was looking for.
Organisation not his forte.
I know he knew my birthday.

Some of your friends can't eat.
Others stand by the buffet the whole time
because at least there is something to talk about there.

Janet organised the spread,
went with sandwiches in the end,
two types of bread,
couple of quiches.

She didn't want to admit it
but Cathy on Mumsnet had been right about not having potato salad.
It would have been a mess.

She went on there because she thought
her choices were beginning to look too much like party food.

Julie in Stoke said,
As long as the person didn't die tragically young I'd say party food is fine.
Jean in Doncaster added, *I always think soup and a sarnie is hard to beat.*

Do you, Jean? Even at a funeral?
I'd say that's fairly easy to beat, if I'm honest.
I ate a plate of raw aubergine once
and I'd still choose that over pretty much anything
that means a mate has to die before I can eat it.
Just a thought, *Jean.*

Sally from Surrey commented six months later to say,
*I know it's probably been and gone,
but did you even consider cheese straws?
Actually deceptively easy to make.*
Thanks, Sally.

You brother suggested getting Alphabetti Spaghetti
so guests could spell out your name on their plates.
Everyone laughed a bit, so he pretended it had been a joke.

No one really mentions what you looked like.
It's almost as if that's not what they liked you for,

as if they would be grieving whatever your waist size
or muscle mass or skin smoothness.
As if they are missing you blindfold.

It's almost as if your body was irrelevant.

Do you ever wonder what you might be remembered in?
Which clothes you might be buried in?
The final image.
The last snap.
Do people plan that?

Perhaps they'll remember me in blue or green?
Or the jacket that was almost definitely once curtains.
Maybe I'll become all the jumpers that people say are nice but also a bit 'mumsy'.
Maybe I will live on in the jacket I bought to combat always getting called 'mumsy'…
Will I be remembered in a hat?
Or a scarf?
Or boots?
Do corpses wear shoes?
I've never looked.
Literally, how do they choose?
A few hair grips in my pocket for good measure, surely?

Which picture will they use to sum me up?
They might use the one that says
she loved animals
or children
or she always felt at home near water,
or the one that screams *she was her mother's daughter.*
Maybe there'll be a mix-up and they'll end up with a picture of Julia Roberts as Erin Brockovich.
That is always a hilarious conversation.

Maybe they'll want to remember me for *having a good time,*
having a glass of wine
but much preferring tea,
or for *always smiling a bit too aggressively.*
Maybe I'll be remembered as *windswept and interesting.*
I mean, really, they could say *anything.*

Does it matter?
Do we remember these things?
I've created so many versions,
I don't know which one they'll bury.
I'm not sure I can care.
I don't know the names of all my great-grandparents.
I don't remember my granddad's voice anymore.
How long will a memory of a scarf last?

But this stuff.
These things.
They matter at the time.
I know that.
I've spent years etching meaning into tat.
I've spent hours between these piles.
To keep, to chuck, to keep or… I get stuck.
Maybe there's some silver, sewn in the lining,
maybe this is where a memory is hiding.
Will I remember why all this was important in five years?
Will I miss it?

It's a tiring decision to make.
So sometimes I postpone bin day
to the next, to the next, to the next,
I don't know if I'll need this,
to the next, to the next, to the next,
would they want me to keep this,
to the next, to the next day.

Stop.

I don't need you to do this.
I don't want to put you through this.
Please remember me in whatever you need.
Tell yourself I loved trifle if you really fancy custard.
Say my favourite colour was yellow
if you want to remember me in mustard.
I'll be there.
If it keeps your dreams light, if it makes the grey bright.
If you lose my scarf, it's fine.
I've lost five;
it would've happened in time.
Don't convince yourself it lessens your love.
Your remembering will be double enough.
Lucky me if someone cares that much. I I have a watch?
Hair up, hair down?

The guests are leaving now.
Scattering themselves back across the country like dandelions.

Janet clingfilms the sandwiches
but bins the salad because no one needs limp lettuce
when they're grieving.

She wraps a piece of Battenberg and puts it in her bag for later.
It was your favourite, so she doesn't want to waste it,
but she knows if she ate it now, she would hardly taste it.

Dogless Dave takes a couple of cocktail sausages home out of habit,
saving them for the dog he buried years ago.

There are cards everywhere.
It could have been a christening.
If you didn't know.

Sorry and *beautiful* waft through the air
like Febreze, masking the odour of that which goes unsaid.

I have transcripts of MSN conversations somewhere.
There's a bashful Bebo account in my name out there.
I don't tweet very frequently,
but that's still more than my dad did. I'm sure that he
would have thought it was a website about birds
for longer than would be endearing.
I can almost hear him.

But now all of that outlives us,
what happens to that stuff?
Gmail or Hotmail can be accessed so that your family can use all your
10% off this or free shipping on that.
Yahoo – no can do, it goes with you. I never knew.
Facebook becomes a memorial page if proof of death is provided.
Dropbox does not have a death policy – they just delete accounts
after long periods of inactivity.
In Dropbox terms, I guess I have already died.
Several times.
Myspace… Myspace did technically die before us
but someone did CPR and it is on life support.
To be continued.

Most of us will have written hundreds, thousands of messages
on this and that, from her, to him:
smoke signals disguised as pleasantries.
Sometimes they crack the cryptics,
send out search parties.
On other days, our words are flares mistaken for stars
and we ride it out alone.

For all this talking we do with our fingers
and capturing of so many images,
are our outlines stronger?
Do our shadows stay for longer
after we have turned the corner?
Are they adding to the summary?
I'm not sure there's a sum of me forming on there.
I am tagged in 603 photos on Facebook.
I don't look worried in a single one.
I don't look confused, or angry, or hopeful.
I look ecstatic. Always.

So when you say *smile* and I don't immediately
I'm just thinking how I want you to think of me.
Because at the moment I guess I am in knitted hats, pictures of cats
and 603 versions of that face –
I'd like to equal more than that.

Pictures are taken down and slideshows are turned off.
It happened.
Everyone said you would have loved it.
Said it was very fitting.

I've heard people say that after weddings as well.
But I've yet to go to a funeral that took two years of planning
and cost as much as a small house.

But both work out fine, both make people cry.
In a way they're both just parties.
And so is life.
We don't remember getting the invite
but we're here now
and nobody wants leave early into the night.

Like a party
we always assume the best bit of life
is a few minutes away.
We want all of our friends to stay for the cake,
a speech, a game and peals of laughter
as someone takes out a lifetime of anger
on a beautiful piñata.
Nobody wants to have to go
when the pizzas come out
or that song comes on –
we've all got one.

Maybe I can say this because
I've not seen the small hours yet.
I've not had to watch every single person leave,
go on to the next party like some VIPs.
Somehow the music is still fresh for me,
but I bet it loops eventually;
there are only so many notes.

Maybe it's harder to stay and be the sage
amongst the young,
like being the only sober one,
harder than slipping out before the cake,
before you're the last one at the wake.
There are only so many candles
you can blow out before it becomes really dark.
I don't envy that part.

Maybe it'll be me.
Maybe, out of everyone I know,
I'll have the cruel task of being the last.
Since being small, I've dreaded that.

Being bereaved as a child
is a bit like realising Father Christmas isn't real, again.
Magic disappears as you are smacked
around your forming skull
with the realisation that this is not the end of it.
If there's no Santa, there can't be a tooth fairy either,
or gnomes in the garden,
or a bunny at Easter.

It is the pricking of your thumbs saying
there is more to come.
More funerals. More deaths. More watching last breaths.
You realise much too soon you are in death's waiting room
with everyone you love
and this is just the beginning of pain.

Cesare De Giglio

Let us know, OK?
What?
You know.
No.
If there's anything we can do.
There isn't.
Anything at all.
There isn't.
Are you sleeping?
Sometimes.
Are you seeing someone?
Loads of people.
Someone to talk to too?
Loads of people.
We could go out sometime?
Yeah, maybe.
Or just stay in…
Yeah, maybe.
We could do some art, make that collage.
Do you want to make a collage?
No, I just thought you might, you know—
Not really.
Sure. That's fine.
Are you taking any, you know…
What?
You know.
No.
Have you tried lavender?
Probably.
Have you tried meditation?
Yes.
And?
Still sad.
Have you thought about cutting out dairy?
Dairy does strange things to your mind…
Are you OK financially?
No.
Oh.
Have you thought about a bench? Or a plaque?
No.
Or a tree?
No.

Doesn't have to be a tree, I suppose.
Maybe a plant?
What plant?
Anything, I guess.
A cactus?
Well, if you think a cactus—
Not really.
OK.
Are you eating?
Sleeping?
Exercising?
Breathing?
Are you doing much breathing?
Give me a call.
Just let me know how you're doing.
Any time, OK?
OK.
Thank you.

Your family won't remember the journey home.
They step over the sinkhole in the doorway and carry on.

The hole won't always gape
but it won't go away.

It becomes a dip in the floor
that brings life back to death

every time they shut the door.
Reminds them the doormat once had home written across it;
now there are just marks that used to be a word.

They close the door
and hang their coats on top of yours in the hall.
The house becomes aglow.
From outside, nobody would know.

When you look out over the city at night,
do you ever imagine a person inside every light?

Every glimmer on the skyline
the sum of a lifeline.
That's what I do.
I've been watching them flickering
and picturing every you
shimmering,
spinning,
dimming.

You're all feeling so much
as you miss those lights
that used to keep your patch bright.
I can hear you screaming some nights.

And I wonder where you look for their embers.
What are we doing with all this?
Is it helping you remember?
Where do they dwell?
I'm listening. Tell.

Your family wake up wishing a hangover would cloud the clarity.
They eat lasagne for breakfast because there are seven in the kitchen,
and Janet has just texted to say she's bringing one later.
Well-wishers' words ring around their heads.
The best fade quickly;
the advice on how to feel or how to deal
fills the holes where pain is supposed to sit,
scars like only care can.

Your belongings become an installation
unknowingly installed by you.
The position of your coat.
The book half-read.
The little note.
Your family review the exhibition internally.
Inferring meaning, intention,
before working out where to store the exhibits.

What happens to it now?
Some want it gone.
Show's over.
Some want to hang it on their walls.
Others can't decipher their own reaction yet
and opt for the limbo of the loft,
the comfort of a box.

Taking things apart is never easy.
The deconstruction might cause new storms
as they clash over interpreting what you wanted,
which is like choosing a plaster cast for a broken leg
because it is not what you wanted.
Cannot be, really.

I was just wondering if you got the frame I left?
Yeah, I did, thank you. Sorry, I meant to ring… I—
Oh, no worries, no, yeah, just glad to, yeah.
It's really nice.
Have you put that picture in it?
Not yet, no.
Could be a different one. I don't mind.
Yeah, maybe.
So many lovely pictures.
Yeah.
Just thought, you know, nice to frame some properly.
Yeah, thanks.
Make it special.
It was really kind. Thank you.
You're welcome. You just call if you need… OK?
I will. I will, thank you.

Sometimes I still feel loss under my nails
or at the nape of my neck.

I bite it out.
Tug it off.
Don't try it.

It leaves you with broken nails, a bald patch
and grief still under your skin.

Sometimes it comes to the surface,
a spot that reminds me of things –
I don't think I ever called him.

It's not dramatic, he didn't have a phone,
I'd never been away from home,
but now there is no one to interrupt Mum when she calls.

And when I have good news,
bad news, sorries, thank-yous,
there is always a call I can't make,
always things I want to share
that go sour between my ribs.

Under the stuff, the things,
the traces of fingerprints,
we leave behind all the feelings
that would have come our way.

Whenever we go, there would have been more –
tears, love, anger, joy,
we leave that.
Those that would have given it wear it on their backs.

They cannot pass it on; it was already named for you.
They have to find a place to plant it
whilst they grow anew.
New love, new anger and tears.
That's what takes time, months, years.
It's not healing. It's growing again.

You cannot put a square peg in a round hole.
You make a new peg.

This is the space I have found
to plant the love of a father
I wasn't meant to keep.

I'm calling him for the first time.
These pages are his answerphone,
taking a pretty hefty voicemail.
It took me a while to pick up the handset.

I said I'd never write about the stuff between my ribs
or my grief-shaped bracelet.
It's not that I couldn't face it –

I thought I got it out like a splinter, at eleven,
scribbling earnestly on notepaper with cats on.
My first poem was called
'Daddy is dead and I don't know what to say about that'.
I think she is the version of me I like the most.

I thought that since then he was writing himself
in the lines in my face,
in my dimples and mouth,
that I wouldn't have to spell any of it out.

But to even think of legacy,
I had to dust off the one closest to me.

And somehow he's in every line
and so am I.
Not forever, and that's just fine.

I wanted to know where my dad lives,
where his memory exists.
Somehow, it's not in the boxes, the things,
any of this.
I wanted it to be.
It would make things neater.
But sometimes you have to swallow pills, don't you?
Without making them sweeter.

Really, he's been on the tip of my tongue
all along,
in the back of my mouth.
I guess by talking
I'm letting him out.

As the days go by
your family are getting to know you again.
At their own pace, in their own space.

You played a different role for each of them in life,
parent, colleague, friend.
How can they be expected to grieve through the same lens?

Your brother is running a marathon,
your mum turns your clothes into cushions,
Ben hasn't said your name yet.

Janet has started an online blog about funeral food
called 'Tasteful Tables'.
Dogless Dave has finally got a new dog and named it after you.
He enjoys shouting your name in the park.

Your sister wants to join in on the marathon,
but she literally can't run half a mile;
does this mean she doesn't love you?
She thinks it might, so she gets a tattoo.

People write to you on Facebook.
Your mum loves that.
Your dad hates that.
There is a charity in your name.
An aunt has planted a tree.
Some friends are doing a skydive.

Jenny from work has changed your job title
so she doesn't actually have to replace you.
Your mug is still in the staff room.
A new employee will use it eventually
and no one will say anything.

There is a recording of your last voicemail.
Someone might have one of your kidneys.
And you will be bloody missed.
Even the parts we said made you a prick.
And we will see you everywhere for a bit.

Song: 'Stranded' by Sam Lunn.

Epilogue

Written September 2002

Daddy is dead now and I don't know what to say about that.
Never did an evil person live on earth he said.
Never did an evil mother give birth he said.
To say that it takes a man so special, so strong,
So why couldn't that special man live long?

Why Daddy, why me? Why anybody, but why Daddy?
Why her, why him? Why has the light gone so suddenly dim?
He said he loved me as much as a pile of pennies
And I wish he could know
I still love him as much as the wind and snow.

Daddy is dead now and I don't know what to say about that.
Never did an evil person live on earth he said.
Never did an evil mother give birth he said.
To say that it takes a man so special, so strong,
So why couldn't that special man live long?

The people he spoke with had hurt or killed,
The people he spoke with no longer had the will
To live.
But once to him they had spoken
He forgave all that, knew their hearts had been broken.
Never did an evil person live on earth he said.
Never did an evil mother give birth he said.
To say that it takes a man so special, so strong,

So why couldn't that special man live long?
He talked to them until their hearts mended.
Then (maybe) he knew his mission had ended.
Daddy is dead now, and that's all I can say about that.

Another bloody survey…

What's the date today? February 21st 2018

What's the weather like? It's cloudy and threatening to rain. I went out without coat or jacket all day yesterday for the first time this year. Not wearing a coat is my favourite outfit.

Where are you? In a room in North London that I rent. I'm not quite sure why I'm here or how long I want to stay, but I'm trying to enjoy it for what it is. It's warm and safe and has a nice fireplace and a view of the bit of the garden that cats come just to go to the toilet in.

If you were planning a celebration of your life right now:

- **What music would you choose?** I'd probably include Flight of the Conchords, John Shuttleworth, Radiohead, Bon Iver, London Grammar and Bob Dylan. If in doubt I would let my brother choose; I always got my music from him anyway. And poems. I'll turn down some pages.
- **Would you be happy for them to be playing the *Match of the Day* theme tune?** I would be very surprised, but NO.
- **What would people be wearing?** Whatever they feel comfortable in. But no Crocs or fleeces, unless it's in a field. I just don't trust them. I don't know why.
- **What would everyone eat?** Lots of vegetables and lots of cake. Not necessarily at the same time, but a good carrot cake does cover a lot of bases if you're pushed for time, doesn't it?
- **What would you definitely NOT like to happen?** No meat, please – one funeral is enough for one day, isn't it?

If your bed was a box, what would you like it to be made of? I've always tried so hard with recycling – it would be a shame to stop now. Cardboard, please. Maybe everyone could write on it? I always wanted one of those casts… but without the broken arm bit.

Are there any of your possessions you would like someone specific to have? I would like Sam to have all the colourful things he used to borrow when we lived together. I would like all of my brilliant writer friends to give my books out to people they think would love them.

What would you like to tell someone that you haven't managed to yet? My brother has always been the funniest person I have known.

If this was your last form of communication, what would you like to say? Talk more often to more people. My favourite bits of life have generally been chats. Thanks for all the brilliant ones you have ever had with me; I will take them all with me.

Your turn…

Please, please photocopy this, give it to people you know, pour your favourite drink and jot down whatever comes into your head without thinking too much. Change the questions or change the answers as time goes on and new music is made.

What's the date today?

What's the weather like?

Where are you?

If you were planning a celebration of your life right now:

- What music would you choose?

- Would you be happy for them to be playing the *Match of the Day* theme tune?

- What would people be wearing?

- What would everyone eat?

- What would you definitely NOT like to happen?

If your bed was a box, what would you like it to be made of?

Are there any of your possessions you would like someone specific to have?

What would you like to tell someone that you haven't managed to yet?

If this was your last form of communication, what would you like to say?

Any other notes?

Seams

When Dead Was My Favourite Colour

At eleven I took Dead out of its box,
spread it onto my palette,
learnt how to splatter it across a conversation,
began to like its uncomplicated shade.
I never used Lost, Asleep, Passed or Heaven.
I watched others dab them onto skies
that always seemed cloudier than mine.
Dead was the only hue I knew how to use.
Much later I would unbox Grief,
mix it with water and recreate the closest colour
to the sky I had been trying to describe.

What Not to Bury

They gave words to me like oranges,
told me my sadness was the smallest in the family,
told me to keep it undercover, underground,
under wraps.
I peeled off the good intentions,
turned them into compost,
absorbed the lot.

If they'd known
what their words would grow
they would have stuck with clichés.

Upstairs

On the fifth day, he was moved upstairs
to a room with a window
and no machines.

After,
I slept on the window ledge
in my purple, velvet *Harry Potter* top.
Gold embellishment
prominent enough to show allegiance,
subtle enough not to make me one of those girls.

I woke as my mother washed him,
closed my eyes again,
did not watch.

I whispered to Erin
that I hoped this never happened to her.
Two years later,
I would write a poem to sit by her dad's body.

We were drawn together, her and I,
by our shared name
and our parents' love of chickpea casserole.
By our dads' singing to us,
by singing to our dads' ethical coffins.

Wearing the maturity cloak
from my dressing-up box,
I thought she was too young.
She was.
We were.
We would be called so now.
We would laugh at that,
as we fiddle with the definition of *daughter*
we hold in our laps.

Billy

Our cat sat on my dad's bag for days.
That nonchalant poignancy only animals can muster.
I would have joined him, if it had been bigger.
It must have been unpacked eventually.

Vegetarian

There are many reasons.
I've used them all.
Read the books, watched the films.
But for me, honestly?
I don't like death
and I do like food.

Phyllis

These streets would have me believe they held you lightly,
that there was always this much laughter on market days.

I look hard for you in your once paper shop, now fancy café,
but all I can smell is marzipan and ambition.

I wish I could buy you the biggest bun, drizzled with understanding,
watch your face as the sugar dissolves and you take in the view –

its gaudy change. There is no prostitute living above your flat these days.
There are no poisonous signs on doors,

your life is not piled on the street.
You have been painted over, revamped, whitewashed,

buried in the window box, so I have to find you where I always have:
in that almost smiling photograph,

in the jacket I am sorry for never being slim enough to wear
and in the airborne image of us meeting on the bridge between generations,

throwing sticks over the side into the current of your pain.

George

i

I believed the story of his falling,
always standing behind yellow lines
in case I was unlucky   like him.

ii

I have never accepted the city he rejected
as home.
I try to make it fit like a second-hand shoe,
insoles and grips   but still it rubs.

iii

Fifty years later, I go to the platform,
a woman asks me directions,
I don't notice the train arrive.

Did he know how many nightmares
he would turn up in?
Or were all platforms empty to him?
Even in rush hour   even at Oxford Circus?

Edna

By the time I could hug back your arms had lost their motive,
had stopped clapping, stopped sewing, stopped squeezing.

By the time I looked for you your eyes had lost their focus,
were stuck replaying jumbled videos of the old days.

If I'd lived fifty miles closer, been born ten years earlier,
I would remember you for more than your frayed edges
and rows of thimbles,

for more than the glass table I always tried to avoid,
for more than shooing cats from the garden.

I would look at the photographs now and recognise
the grimace of a grandma who protested the gender pay gap
before it was even called that,
pearls glinting, heels high, hair unquestionable,
knitting the memories I only saw unravel.

Ken

I think I remember you
telling us about the time you had to clean
behind your eyes. I retell it, gorier each time,
until the past is a story and you are a god.

I think I remember you
feeding her chocolates in her chair,
hoping the taste of a favourite might stir up
some recognition,
no falter when it didn't.

I think I remember you
crying once, but the background is unfocussed
and if you cleaned behind your eyes
I doubt there were many tears left.

I think I remember you,
smile bright, jumper beige, extra custard,
put your wallet away,
as someone I maybe, might have
read poems to one day.

The Trick

Remembering is the only magic trick I know.
I go to pull you out of my sleeve like a handkerchief,
afraid each time that the trick will fail:
abracadabra – nothing there.

Little One

If I could, I would not tell my younger a self a thing.
I would study her face and try to mimic the bits
where a father lives. I would hold her hand,
feel the imprint of his, ask her everything in a blink,
watch her read the lines on my forehead,
realising how smooth hers is.
I would smile at her smile, tie my tongue in a bow
and not speak about the tricks her face will play.
I would hug her hard until she set up home in my spine,
adding an inch to my height with every stretch of her grin.

Fossils

When they dig me up in years to come,
they will find a cliff face
covered in imprints of everyone I have ever known.

You will all be there, all of you,
swirling and cracked and intricate.

A child will squeal with excitement and pride.
She will take the memories you pressed into my bones
home in a bucket.

We will be examined, admired
and misunderstood
a thousand times more.

It keeps me going somehow,
to know that even the bad days
will make beautiful fossils.

If You Were Not Dead

I wouldn't feel the need to have a vanilla slice on your birthday.
There wouldn't be a collage of you in my room.
I would measure life with a different tape.
I wouldn't search for your reflection in your brother's face
or listen for you in his laugh.
I wouldn't wonder who might be dead every time my phone rings;
I might even turn it off at night sometimes.
I would probably say Father's Day is stupid and commercial.
I wouldn't have said the word *dead* so many times
and I probably wouldn't have learnt to drive.
Our gravy would be so much better
and my days would still be made by you letting me dip the bread in.
I wouldn't unpick my feelings for people
by imagining my reaction to their deaths.
I wouldn't worry about how much I think about you.
I wouldn't snap a twig every time someone says, *No one's died!*
My brother wouldn't have dug a grave or carried you on his shoulders.
My mum wouldn't have had to do all the parent-taxi trips
and your room, her room, probably wouldn't be pink.
I would have no idea that last breaths can sound so conflicted.
There would be no blankets made of your clothes
and everything would be a little bit louder.
I wouldn't know how heavy love can be when it is returned to sender.
I would know the pattern of your pride,
without having to take other people's word for it.
This would be a blank page. In a blank book.

Steve Stephens

Thank you to Arts Council England for the pennies.

Thank you to the Roundhouse (especially Rachel, Josie, Victoria and Linda) for the space, support and encouragement to make this into a thing from the off.

Thank you, Roberta Zuric, for being so brilliant and open right from that very first coffee and for asking all the right questions.

Thank you, Sam Lunn, for the beautiful music.

Thank you, Emma Higham, for the excellent input.

Thank you, Lewis Buxton, Sara Hirsch and Jess Davies for your time and the invaluable feedback on the poems in 'Seams'.

Thank you, Lowenna Melrose, for chatting so generously and letting me record it.

Thank you, Peter Hose, for the support and encouragement to start performing poems and to keep writing them.

Thank you, Erin Mckee, for being my 'other' one all this time, for chatting so openly and for being so kind about some truly mixed shows over the years.

Thank you, Lyall Stephens, for the patience, technical wizardry, 99% of my music collection and the love of Alan Partridge.

Thank you, Mum, for the baked goods, excellent post and all the love.

Thank you, Dad, for being such a loving, open man and father who is still providing all this inspiration fifteen years later. We all wish you were here.

Thank you to all the poets, performers and makers who keep creating work that inspires, questions, tickles and stuns me.

Thanks also to the many people around them who make that possible.

Thanks to you for reading a book with a relatively sombre title. I hope you had a little smile along the way too.

THE OTHER SIDE OF THE DOOR

Harriette Lewis

MINERVA PRESS
LONDON
ATLANTA MONTREUX SYDNEY

THE OTHER SIDE OF THE DOOR
Copyright © Harriette Lewis 1998

All Rights Reserved

No part of this book may be reproduced in any form
by photocopying or by any electronic or mechanical means,
including information storage or retrieval systems,
without permission in writing from both the copyright
owner and the publisher of this book.

ISBN 0 75410 352 8

First Published 1998 by
MINERVA PRESS
195 Knightsbridge
London SW7 1RE

Printed in Great Britain for Minerva Press

THE OTHER SIDE
OF THE DOOR

Dedication

Dedicated to my husband, His Honour Judge Bernard Lewis, who had to be neglected so that I could find the time to trawl through all those casebooks in search of social problems which were not due exclusively to poverty.

Foreword

Fifteen Years of 'Social' Climbing

It was 1946. I was staring at three middle-aged women. Actually they were staring at me. I was overawed. I had crossed the floor of a very large empty room in London's County Hall and they were seated behind a huge desk on a raised platform. Although I had accepted an invitation to sit down I felt more like turning tail and getting away as far as possible from those women. I was certainly regretting my impulsive response to the accomplished speaker who had planted the idea in my head that I wanted to be a voluntary School Care Committee worker.

The woman seated in the middle of the trio barked, 'Why do you want to do this work?'

The question was totally unexpected and I was nonplussed. I remember asking myself that question as I searched for something to say. Then I blurted out, 'I don't really know. I like people and I do love children.'

She didn't even consult her colleagues. Smiling faintly she said, 'You'll do.'

And that was the beginning of fifteen years of voluntary work in a very poor neighbourhood of London which had had its share of Hitler's bombs.

I soon learned how important it was to like people and to be fond of children. The whole system worked on that basis. Children's School Care Committees began at the turn of the century. They arose out of the old Poor Law Relief Committees. Their aim was to deal with all matters affecting school children because it was recognised by a few women, who had a sense of civic responsibility, that *a child could not benefit from free education if it was cold and hungry.* By 1929 a nucleus of professionals steered a vast army of volunteers who were playing an ever-increasingly important part in the welfare of children in London's schools. This encompassed, incidentally, the welfare of their parents.

Before the war there were five thousand volunteers. By 1954, there were only about three thousand. They had to deal with far more problems which caused a tremendous drive to recruit the right kind of volunteer at a time when there were fewer men and women able to spare time. Perhaps it should be said that if money is surplus to requirements, it is easy to give it to charity. It is not a sacrifice. On the other hand, to give up some of one's leisure is a sacrifice and therefore a high form of charity… and it can really be rewarding to the giver.

Soon after I began to work in the catchment area of my school, I came to the conclusion that the area consisted of nothing but tenement houses full of endless steps. I had to climb steep, narrow staircases, often rickety and dangerous and, at the end of those stairways, there would be a closed door. If it did open, it would open no more than a few suspicious inches.

Behind that closed door were all the hopes and all the fears, all the emotions and all the passions of people whose lives were not cluttered with too many ideas of refinement. They lived without excessive inhibitions. They were, perhaps, more real and more human than most of us. But the door at the end of those stairs was firmly closed. Few

I was not the only climber of those steep, narrow stairs I discovered, nor the only habitual knocker-on-the-door. The rent collector had been a 'regular' before me. Both he and I had something in common. Apart from climbing and knocking, that is, like him I wanted something. That is what the parents thought, at any rate, and I had to convince them, without any shadow of a doubt, that for their children's sake I was on their side of the door... that I had come to give, not to take away.

There was an occasion when, long before I sat down to record the events described in the stories which follow, I was established in Mrs X's muddled kitchen. Untidy though she was, she had an amiable and hospitable nature.

Her kitchen on the top floor of a tenement building was comfortably warm. I had climbed all the way up those stairs to enquire why she had not taken her small Albert to be provided with new spectacles. As it happened, Mrs X was one of those who knew that nobody paid me to fret about her children, not even little Albert. Our friendship had ripened over her many troubles and those of her children, and she knew that I could have no other motive than to help her with her difficulties.

Her excuses for not bringing little Albert to the school clinic did not deceive me. She knew that too. At last, she admitted that it had been due to her usual muddle-headedness. She was, as always, contrite.

Now, sitting in the front row of his class because he could not see the blackboard, little Albert had been coming to school for three weeks without spectacles. His defective eyesight was one of my constant worries. Albert's broken glasses were never his fault, according to him. As he managed to damage them quite frequently, I knew better. His position in the class was giving him other troubles. Not being too popular with his contemporaries at the moment, for various reasons not to be divulged to his mother, he was strangers ever really got behind it, and I had to earn my passage.

At first I thought it would be easy. If that closed door opened, I would put on my brightest smile. Then, with what I thought would be a disarming opening gambit, I used the formula, 'I'm the new Voluntary Care Committee worker at Mavenna Street School.' It got me precisely nowhere except to establish my quasi-official status with the London County Council and my concern with the children attending the school. I began to get a clearer understanding of what lay behind my interrogator's question at County Hall. Liking people and smiling at them was never going to get me behind closed doors. I learned that lesson pretty soon.

My first discovery was also that it was by no means always wise to lay too much stress on being 'voluntary'. To some it meant that all this climbing, wholly gratis and for nothing, showed that I 'ought to have my head examined'. Some hoped or suspected that, bored with a life of ease and luxury, I had come to dispense largesse. Others, more philosophical, gave me the impression that they thought there was no accounting for tastes. With quite a few, only respect for official status prevented those inches from being rudely shut again!

To prevent the door from closing was a very long way, however, from getting inside, from even getting into the 'parlour' where, in that part of London, life was not *lived* and which rarely held any secrets. I was far from getting into the kitchen and its intimate happenings, and still farther from getting into the becurtained bedroom.

All my social calls concerned a child, of course. Only too often, however, the cause of the trouble seemed to lie with the parents. It didn't take long to realise that unless I could gain admittance, I would not effect the purpose for which I had called.

engaged in rearguard actions with his tormentors. All this was scarcely in his best interests and I was on the point of extracting a firm promise from his mother to take him to the clinic when there was a loud rat-tat-tat on the front door.

"Ush, ducky,' whispered Mrs X conspiratorially, 'that'll be 'Is Nibs! Don't let 'im 'ear you. Bit be'ind, I am, this week. Ain't got the bloomin' rent.'

I 'ushed. It was not part of my business to lighten the burden of my co-knocker on the door, whose work in that neighbourhood even in the days of accommodation scarcity could hardly be a sinecure. I stifled my conscience.

As soon as 'His Nibs' gave up trying and we heard his footsteps retreating, little Albert's mother and I got back to the evergreen subject of her son. Mrs X had just given me one of her faithful promises to keep my next appointment for him at the clinic, when we heard a commotion outside which 'ushed us again.

'His Nibs', it seemed, had failed to get a reply from Mrs Y who inhabited the ground floor of the house next door. This was not surprising. I knew that this was the day, and about the time, Mrs Y did her weekly wash in the public baths. If, after all these years, the rent collector still did not know this, and still used his feet instead of his head, it was not my job to enlighten him.

In all probability, Mrs Z as well as Mrs Y would be at the baths having a good natter while both thumped out the dirt from their 'smalls'. More than likely, Mrs Z was equally behind with the rent.

The commotion outside persisted. We listened to it and heard the neighbours ranging themselves on the side of the defaulters.

'No, I don't know w'en Mrs Y will be back…'

'No, I carn't say if Mrs X works. She don't tell me 'er business, she don't.'

"Fraid I ain't 'eard if Mr Z's back on full time yet…'

We heard the footsteps recede. He had gone, but not from my mind.

'Mrs X,' I said reproachfully, now that the immediate problem of Albert was settled, 'you really are the limit! Come now, out with it! What *have* you been up to again? You know very well you only postpone the evil moment. The rent will have to be paid.'

She looked at me, ashamed yet defiant. As a result of our long acquaintance, I knew how much Mr X earned and how much he gave to her. I even knew how much he picked up 'on the side'. Together we worked it all out again. It was over a little matter of inadequate budgeting, not poverty, which I was meeting more infrequently those days, that I came to know Mrs X so well.

I knew her failings as well as her virtues. We had been friends long enough for me to sort out this very personal problem. Whether the deficit was due to tobacco or the tally man, the pub or the pictures, Mrs X knew that I knew. She also knew that I never condemned her, which made her more willing to trust my judgement. All she lacked was the strength of will to stick to a budget. The only axe I had to grind was the same as her own… our interest in little Albert and the rest of her brood. Knowing this she, like so many others, had let me into her kitchen.

While we were busily engaged in sorting out Mrs X's finances, I made a mental note to call upon Mrs Y and Mrs Z. Their Jacks and their Jills also attended my school and, sooner or later, the consequences of their mothers' peccadilloes were going to be visited upon my children. And so, although he never knew it, I found myself compelled to give that other climber-of-stairs and knocker-on-doors a helping hand.

So it had to be, too, with the 'cruelty man'.

To be sure, my friend the NSPCC inspector got inside those closed doors when the need arose. He got in by virtue of his status but the 'cruelty man' in that neighbourhood was measured by the size of his boots. His feet had not shrunk since his retirement from the police force. He was still a 'policeman' to the inhabitants.

He knew, as I did, that in whatever home he entered the occupants would use all their mental talents to conceal from him that which he had come to find out. He knew, too, the bond which existed between School Care Committee workers and their flocks and, in their own interests, he frequently enlisted their cooperation because fear is not always the most appropriate deterrent to cruelty. At the same time, he was very conscious that he and they had to travel their separate ways.

He appears at least once in my stories as a valuable helpmeet but what follows is not written for those who want to read about cruelty to children, nor for those who merely wish to pry into the lives of others. They are true stories, part of our social history. The honorary secretaries of School Care Committees had to direct any hint of the sexual abuse of a child to a special department in County Hall. Our 'helpline' was for the deprived or neglected child. Often this entailed marriage guidance. But if a recent article by a well-known writer in a reputable daily newspaper which was headed 'A Child Won't Learn on an Empty Stomach' is anything to go by, and the key to UK prosperity is in the cry, education, education, education, then maybe that cry should include an appeal to revive a system of School Care Committees. In one hundred years, the wheel seems to have turned full circle.

Harriette Lewis
October 1997

Contents

Motherly Love	15
IQ… or no IQ?	24
Jessie's Crime	32
Monkey Business	50
Sensibility	59
Turn, thou Ghost, that Way…	66
Even as a Hen Gathereth her Chickens…	78

Motherly Love

'And then I sez to 'im, I sez,' Bobby Mellor went on, as he sat beside his hostess in the farmhouse scullery, shelling peas, 'my mum'll be after yer for callin' me such nymes...'

Mary Smith looked at the nine-year-old boy with ill-concealed impatience. For three days she had listened to his incessant chatter and she was reaching the end of her tether.

'Why don't you want to play in the fields, Bobby?' she asked for about the tenth time that morning.

The boy stopped talking for a moment and went on shelling peas. He shook back his untidy hair, sniffed audibly and gazed out of the kitchen window. The warm sun made his wan face seem paler still.

'The men need your help,' continued Mrs Smith encouragingly. 'Bill and Ken are out in the harvest field helping too. Do go and join them.'

The boy looked blank. There seemed no expression in his face at all.

'Oi ain't used to the fields,' he answered candidly. 'Oi ain't no good at it but Oi loikes bein' 'ere wiv you.'

Mrs Smith sighed. A mere three days of Bobby's interminable stories, in which his mother always figured as a kind of heroine, seemed a poor return for her impulsive decision to give a London child a fortnight's holiday in the country.

Bill and Ken had looked forward to having another child to play with them but, apart from the first 'hullos', the children had little to say to the newcomer. They left each morning with the men. Bobby, on the other hand, followed her about, talking – and sniffing – apparently desiring to do nothing else. His expression was as monotonous as his chatter, the only change in his face being a muscular twitch when he sniffed.

'Bobby,' said Mrs Smith testily, her patience snapping, 'I like having you here, but I can't get on with my work with you hanging about. The boys want you to play with them – that's why I invited you – and all you do is sit around the kitchen and follow me about. Now do be a good boy, Bobby,' she coaxed. 'Go out and play in the fresh air.'

Bobby sniffed loudly and Mrs Smith hid her revulsion.

'Oi'll go,' he said quietly, 'but Oi won't be in yer way, Oi won't, reely Oi won't. Oi'll 'elp yer.'

She relented. Together they made beds and swept floors to the drone of Bobby's endless chatter. It was only when the men and the other children came in to dinner and Mrs Smith could listen to the harvest talk, and the merry voices of her own two boys, that she felt relief from the tension which three days of Bobby's company had created. It seemed unreal to her that a mere three days of this child's presence, following her from room to room, constantly sniffing and talking in his cockney voice, could have produced such an effect upon her nerves.

'I'll have to send him back to London, Bill,' she said firmly that night as she lay wide awake, trying to make an exhausted husband listen to her woes. She kept him awake with her vivid, tense description of the boy's effect upon her. 'He's driving me mad,' she went on, 'following me around like a lost dog. It's getting me down. You'd think a nine-year-old boy would want to play with other children. I don't understand him. But I've made up my mind. He'll have to go home. I'll tell the church committee tomorrow that I can't stand the boy any longer. It was all a mistake. I simply can't bear another eleven days of this!'

Her sleepy husband made an effort to rouse himself. 'Mary, you can't do that! Think of the kid's parents. He's done nothing wrong. Don't forget, it was all your idea in the first place. I told you we had enough trouble at harvest time with Bill and Ken without adding another youngster. You were all for it. *You* said Bill and Ken would be less trouble. Now you want to send him home!'

The vehemence in her voice, as she answered, startled him.

'Bill, I think I hate that child!'

He was wide awake then. 'You just can't hate a child, Mary, not you! And him such a quiet little chap.'

'I tell you,' she wailed, 'he's getting on my nerves. God, how I wish I'd never had the idea. There's something about his wooden face and his awful sniff that makes me shudder. As for his mother, well, she must be nearly as wonderful as he says she is if she's able to put up with him all the time.'

'Come off it, Mary,' said Bill, settling himself back down. 'Be a love and go to sleep. You'll feel better about him in the morning.'

For a long time Mary Smith listened to his even breathing, desperately searching an escape from the eleven days which lay before her, thinking up impossible schemes, until she too fell asleep.

The next day the sun shone as brightly as ever and the farmhouse kitchen smelt good as the family sat down at the table. Bobby, seated beside Mary Smith, sniffed his way through breakfast, gazed woodenly around him and continued his monologue, addressed to her only, almost from the same point where he had left off the night before.

'So my mum sez to them boys, she sez...'

She was past listening to him any more, as he flitted from one thought to the other. By this time he had given up asking questions. He was content merely to talk, unaware of the fact that his hostess no longer said 'yes' and 'no' at appropriate intervals.

After the men and the boys had departed into the field where, from the windows, she could see them toiling, she began her daily work in the kitchen. Bobby followed her into the scullery, then back into the kitchen, until finally she could bear it no longer.

'Bobby,' she said a little shrilly, putting both her hands to her ears, 'if you don't leave me alone and go away and play with the boys... or help in the fields or... or something, I'll have to send you home to your mother.'

For an instant Mary thought she saw his expressionless face alter as he shook the untidy strands of hair from his forehead.

'Orl right, ma'am,' he answered quietly and went out through the scullery door and into the field beyond.

After that, things were a little better. Mary Smith tried to persuade herself that there was no hint of mournfulness in Bobby's eyes. He had taken her threat seriously, and religiously followed the men into the fields, but at mealtimes he addressed all his remarks to her, and insisted on drying the dishes afterwards.

All the time she was washing them, he talked on and on, and sniffed and sniffed. There was no escape for her from his monologue. He dealt with the minutest details of his life at home. Occasionally he spoke of the other children. Sometimes he referred to his father. As a variation, she had to listen to long stories about the neighbours at home. Always in his stories, his mother emerged with a halo which, in some indescribable way, contrasted with the mechanical sniff.

She found it harder and harder to 'like' him, let alone 'love' him. When he turned his little wooden face up to be kissed at night after saying his prayers with the others, Mrs

Smith closed her eyes, pecked his cheek and hated herself for that inward dislike.

Mary Smith had meant well but the fortnight she had promised the child seemed endless. Her heart was a good deal lighter when she awoke on the morning he was due to leave. She tried to dismiss twinges of conscience at the relief she felt that he was going. All the time they were standing on the platform, she tried not to notice the mournful expression in his eyes. His sniffing seemed to her to grow louder by the minute.

Earlier she had salved her conscience by packing a huge parcel of food for his army of brothers and sisters, with something special for his wonderful mother. The last she saw of him – when she waved goodbye from the platform – was his small figure standing at the carriage door, tightly hugging one of the parcels under one arm, plucking with the other hand at the discarded pullover she had given him that morning... and his mournful gaze.

She felt guilty at the relief she experienced watching the departing train. Until she had given hospitality to this strange child she had believed herself to be fond of children. She thought now that there were some children only their mothers could love. Secretly her heart went out to the mother of Bobby.

But in the breast of Bobby, who was watching the fields flash by as the train sped towards London, there was a heavy load.

'Bob Mellor don't cry!' he kept whispering. He had said this to himself so often in the past years... ever since they told him his mother was dead and even more so when his stepmother came to live with his father and showed interest only in her own children.

And the harder he swallowed to stem the rising tears, the more he sniffed until the other occupants of the crowded railway carriage felt, no doubt, that the journey to

London would never end. Eventually the large woman sitting next to him could bear it no longer.

'Little boy,' she said sharply, 'have you no hanky?'

'Nah, ma'am,' replied Bobby woodenly, and sniffed again.

She opened her handbag, extracted a clean handkerchief which she shook from its folds and said loudly, 'Here! Have this one, child! Blow your nose!'

Bobby accepted the proffered gift mechanically, stuffed it in his pocket and sniffed again.

The other passengers must have smiled behind their reading matter. An hour later the journey was over and Bobby was once more sniffing heartily within the bosom of his family who were as indifferent to his return as they had been to his departure.

*

During the first week of the autumn school term, I always received the conduct reports of the children for whom I had managed to find a place for a fortnight's holiday by the sea or in the country. This is what I read:

> Report of the district officer, Fairhope, on Bobby Mellor, aged nine.
>
> He is obedient, well-behaved and quiet mannered. But he is a most nerve-racking child with apparently a perpetual sniff. According to Mrs Smith, in spite of glorious weather, he refused to leave the house. He just sat in the kitchen and never stopped talking. Later she did manage to get him out.
>
> You are earnestly requested *never* to send him again to a private house, as he cannot fall in with the ways of a family and he talks even while he eats.

The Bobby in this report did not fit into my mental picture of him. I knew him to be a somewhat listless child, the removal of whose adenoids had been recommended by the school doctor, but I felt a little impatient with this blanket condemnation. Besides, the reason why I had sought a summer holiday for him was because it would 'build him up' for the proposed removal of his adenoids. His mother had gratefully accepted my idea and had, in fact, saved up the fare money.

I decided to have a word with Bobby. He was standing in a corner of the playground, well away from the other children. Admiring the pullover with which he was fidgeting, I began by asking him who gave him that nice hanky which was sticking out of his trouser pocket.

'A kind lady in the train,' he said.

That was how I learned about the journey home. On his assurance that the compartment was full of passengers, I suppressed a laugh. Smiling broadly, I continued, 'Did you enjoy your holiday?'

'Yes'm.' Only his lips moved in his expressionless face.

'Was the family kind to you, Bobby?'

'Yes'm,' came the answer.

'And Mrs Smith, was she kind to you too?'

A faint recollective smile hovered on the child's lips.

'Oh yes'm, yes'm, she wuz!'

I felt I was getting somewhere.

'Was she like your mum at home?' I persisted.

There was a moment when I thought I saw real emotion flicker across Bobby's pale face. It seemed to me that it flushed suddenly with genuine astonishment.

'Why ma'am,' he replied, 'Mrs Smith's a *real* mum. You see,' he volunteered, 'I tell'd 'er lots of fings. Like a real mum she never onc't said "shut up"!'

I averted my eyes. I didn't want the boy to see the tears that sprang into them.

That evening I wrote a long explanatory letter to Mary Smith, telling her that Bobby's mother had died when he was three years old and that his father had remarried soon afterwards. It was not until I had spoken to Bobby on his return from the farm that I had gleaned the real truth. Until then, his stepmother had managed to convince me that Bobby was as much a child of the family as all her own children. Indeed, all the children of the family, including Bobby, resembled the father physically so that I had come to the conclusion that he was so young when his mother died, he could scarcely be expected to regard his stepmother as anyone other than his mother.

Mrs Smith's reply was very moving. In fact, she wrote the whole story, hiding nothing. She added that she had cried a little when she learned about Bobby's real background.

I decided to waste no time. Taking advantage of that letter, I asked Mary Smith whether she would consider having Bobby again the following summer. Back came these heart-warming words:

Send him to me for Christmas. I'll make sure I have plenty of handkerchiefs and I promise I'll teach him how to use them.

As the years passed, Mrs Smith never forgot Bobby's birthday and always sent Christmas presents. Every summer he spent a fortnight on the farm. Every following autumn, I would find a letter from her in the school medical room. It was after his third summer holiday on the farm that I read:

I think I've nearly cured Bobby of that awful sniff. We play a game every morning called 'handkerchief drill'. The whole family joins in the game. I call 'one-two-three-blow' and we all blow our noses heartily into our hankies.

A terrific clatter from below the window caused me to look up from the letter. The eleven-year-olds had burst into the playground for their morning break as though let loose from a prison. When I spotted Bobby he was contributing lustily to the din. I smiled at the thought of how much Bobby had thawed in the warmth of Mary Smith's motherly love.

'The "hanky-drill"… you may be right, Mary,' I said aloud, 'but I think Bobby doesn't sniff all that much any more because he has discovered the blessed relief of tears.'

IQ... or no IQ?

To me, there is something vaguely strange about this business of calculating intelligence quotients... like trying to divine the occult. I was perfectly happy to divide, merely into three groups, the hundreds of little seekers-after-knowledge who formed the population of my school. They were, by my standards, 'the bright', the 'not so bright' and the 'frankly dull'. There might be a margin of error in this kind of reckoning, but when one hasn't time for IQ assessments, it seemed as good a yardstick as any, both for the children and the adults.

It was, for example, eleven o'clock on a bright wintry morning, during my early days at Mavenna Street School when, still rather innocent as to what my work entailed, I turned into Pilbeck Street with a schedule of three lengthy staircases to climb, a major problem at the end of each, and no thoughts whatsoever in my head concerning different levels of intelligence.

Powdery snow was beginning to settle in the street. The best I could hope for, I remember thinking, was that I should get back into the school before the classrooms disgorged their contents into the playground. If I failed to negotiate that playground before then, about a thousand little fiends, with a variety of IQs, would use me, with varying good natures, as their snowball target. It would be their nature, and not their IQs that would determine the fierceness of the battle which I preferred to avoid.

''Scuse me,' said a panting voice behind me, in a local accent.

I started. In the snow I had not heard the footsteps behind me.

'You're the lady wot looks after the kids at Mavenna Street School, ain't ye?' said the woman I had swung round to face.

At my nod, she moved a little closer and lowered her voice to more confidential tones, although there wasn't a soul in sight.

'Well,' she said, a little breathlessly, having evidently run to catch me up, 'there are three little children all alone in number eleven, with a fire going, too! Their mum leaves them every morning. Goes to the pub, I reckon!'

Indignation welled up in my inexperienced bosom.

'Thank you for telling me,' I said.

'You're welcome!' she replied, and disappeared, grinning like the Cheshire cat, as rapidly as she had appeared. Her personality was not a pleasing one, but I had no reason to question her native intelligence.

I approached the knocker of number eleven with a demeanour which would have done justice to any disciple of the suffragette movement and rapped imperiously. A window above me opened from the top of the house next door and an old woman leaned out and glowered at me.

'She's gorn out!' she snapped. The window slammed before I could reply.

I gave a piece of string hanging from a hole in the door an angry tug. To my surprise, the door opened. This was my first experience of pieces of string hanging from front doors; it was very nearly my last experience of voluntary social work.

Inside there was no other sound but a crackle, the crackle of a fire burning somewhere in this dark cavern of a home. I was frightened, but took a couple of steps into the hall and closed the door behind me. As my eyes became accustomed to the darkness, I realised that a door on the right was slightly ajar. I pushed it open. Except for the flickering of the fire, there was no light in that room at all. No chink of the bright daylight outside penetrated what, I afterwards discovered, was a dark grey army blanket. The silence in the house was eerie.

I called out, 'Is anyone in?'

There was no reply. I knew that all I had succeeded in doing was to give myself additional 'shock' treatment with the sound of my own voice.

I was just turning to go out again when something in what was the darkest corner of the room seemed to move. I panicked, and very nearly fled, when I recognised the outline of the small fair head of a child.

With an effort, I controlled my voice and whispered, 'Are you all in bed?'

Two more fair little heads popped up beside the first. I breathed more evenly, although there was still no answer. I stumbled my way across the floor of the room, almost falling a number of times as I tripped over a variety of impediments, and raised the window blanket a little, admitting a triangle of daylight. In a bed in the corner of the room, solemnly sucking their thumbs, sat three small children bolt upright, their bodies covered by the same kind of dark grey blanket which shrouded the window.

'Are you ill?' I whispered again.

All three heads shook in denial. Clearly they understood, whatever their IQ! Then something happened which made me freeze to the spot where I stood. A watery voice, emanating from a small thin woman who was standing in the doorway, demanded ominously, 'Who are you? How dare you come into my home!'

The three children were still solemnly sucking their hands as the window blanket dropped from my fingers.

Once more, the only light in the room was the glow cast by the fire. The flickering coals picked out the gilt rims of the woman's spectacles. I don't know whether it was the firelight or her hair, but I thought I saw wild, wispy streaks on her face.

One thing, however, was quite certain. I was in a pretty tight corner and, instinctively, I realised that this was no time to begin an IQ assessment. If my rapid estimate of her likely intelligence was right, there was probably only one chance left to me to extricate myself from this appalling situation.

I drew myself up to my full height. She was no more than five feet tall, and my passport has me down as five feet four and a half inches. In a voice that I hoped sounded authoritative, I said, 'How dare you go into public houses at this hour of the day, leaving three children alone in a house with an unguarded fire!'

I glanced at the children out of the corner of my eye. All three sat, still sucking their fingers, like graven images. It occurred to me that it was strange that I should see them so clearly in the darkness, even if my eyes had grown accustomed to it.

The woman stood stock-still. I moved towards her as steadily as I could, remembering the number of objects on the floor. Each time I stumbled, I made what was intended to be an aggressive grunt.

Only as I neared the door did I begin to regain a little confidence.

'Get those children out of bed,' I commanded, 'washed and dressed! Get them into the healthy snow outside, *and* into school!'

By this time I had almost reached the silent creature standing in the doorway. She stepped back into the hall and, by the light of the partly open front door, I caught another glimpse of her colourless countenance. She blinked at me from behind her spectacles.

Mumbling to keep my courage up, I backed towards the street door, feeling for it with my hand behind me. As I made contact with the door, it steadied my trembling and renewed my evaporating courage.

'If I find that this happens again,' I threatened, my escape route now completely safe, 'I shall call the police!'

*

The divisional organiser was kind, most helpful in her advice too, concerning my future tactics, having taken into account the abnormal mentality of the mother, of which, looking back on my experience, there could be little doubt.

The sting lay in her parting words.

'You realise,' she said, with the dignified smile which divides the voice of authority from the well-meaning voluntary worker, 'that if this woman had not been as silly as she is, and had really stood up for her rights, the council would have been obliged to disown you? The Englishman's home is his castle... and you are not entitled to "break and enter"!'

*

Subsequent events showed that I had misled the organiser as well as myself but, first, I made two further mistakes. I informed the school attendance officer and communicated with the NSPCC, to secure the safety of those three children. Fortunately my own IQ began to re-establish itself by continuing to tell me that I should make a second call upon this woman myself.

My reason for this was obscure. On reflection, I attributed it to her speechlessness, but have never been quite sure of this. So I took my courage in both hands and called the following afternoon. This time I knocked politely.

I hoped, as I stood there, that she would not be in, but I was not long left in doubt.

She opened the door and recognised me at once, although her face showed no emotion, hostile or otherwise.

Before I could speak, she addressed me. 'Won't you come in?' she said in a voice plainly indicative of a superior education.

This made me more anxious than I had already been. An educated woman, if mentally disturbed, was likely to be more dangerous. I followed her without a word into the same room in which I had come upon the children.

'I'm sorry about yesterday,' she continued, as she preceded me. The dark grey window shroud hung limply by the side of the frame, and the children had vanished.

'Where are those delightful children?' I asked, as if disappointed at not seeing them.

'Out,' she smiled.

Deciding not to be put off, I said invitingly, 'You have arranged for the older ones to go to school?'

'Please sit down,' was her reply.

I chose a seat near the door. Mental disorders frighten me and I wanted to be certain of keeping my escape exit clear.

There was a strained silence. When she spoke again, I was surprised by the level tone of her small voice.

'I don't know your name,' she said quietly, 'or your vocation, or the capacity in which you called, but you gave me such a shock yesterday that I was speechless. When you had gone,' she added ruefully, 'I thought of all the things I should have said…'

'For instance?' I interrupted, seeking to gain time as it dawned on me that I must indeed have been mistaken about her.

'I should have replied,' she said, in her thin voice, smiling faintly as she spoke, 'if I find you in my home again, it will be I who will call the police!'

I flushed to the roots of my hair.

'What do you mean?' I said, wishing devoutly that I had shown more sense than to make a second call.

'Would you mind if I ask you who you are?' she queried in reply.

I didn't mind. I tried to give her a description of my functions and could hear the shakiness in my own voice. Her eyes narrowed when she heard how I had been informed about the children and had felt impelled to make that entry. As I was talking she moved nearer to me, and my fears returned.

Suddenly she sat down on the edge of the bed, and I backed away a little towards the far side of my chair. One more inch, I speculated, and I'd be on the floor!

In tones almost devoid of emotion, she related her story and, as the painful tale reached its climax, I was no longer in doubt of the value of IQ tests. Had she and I submitted to the usual assessment, there would be now no vestige of doubt as to which of us would have obtained the higher rating!

What she lacked was experience, and money. She did not lack intelligence or courage, or sanity. In her desperation to escape from the miseries inflicted by a habitually drunken husband, she had sought, as a temporary roof over her head, the home of a former domestic help of the family. Coming upon me the day before inside her refuge, she had mistaken me for an agent sent by her husband.

'Each morning,' she concluded her story, 'I must go out if I am to obtain employment. Janice is seven, and very sensible. Mary is five, but the baby is only two. Our former maid has to work for her living. If I send the girls to school, there is no one to look after the baby. As soon as I get work – a librarian's job isn't easy to find – I shall be able to put Jonathan into a nursery.'

Her lips trembled, and a faint smile flitted across her pale, thin face again.

I realised that I was now sitting square on that chair, staring at her, our roles completely reversed. My mistake appeared so gross and unjustified that she might well have regarded me as the mental case. There must have been something in my expression which made her add mirthlessly, 'Idiotic situation I have put myself in, don't you think?'

I wanted to laugh and knew that it was from relief, but the nightmarish thought of all the wheels I had set in motion sobered me. At all costs, I had to act quickly in order not to cause her more trouble.

Aloud I said, 'There must be a way to help you...'

'A job is all I need,' she replied with dignity.

'Yes!' I cried, as the idea struck me, 'that's it! The chairman of the local education committee... he'll have the answer. Mind you,' I continued, now permitting myself to chuckle with relief, 'he can hardly read or write, but he is an exceedingly shrewd man of affairs, and I am sure he will be able to help us.'

Despite her troubles, she laughed. I felt that we had got to know each other and that, if I refrained from jumping to righteous conclusions, I might not do so badly in an IQ test after all. Nevertheless, I privately decided, as a measure of safety, never to submit to one.

Jessie's Crime

The story of Jessie has no real ending, and yet I like to regard it as one of my successes. I knew, before I left the scene of all those years of voluntary social work, that Jessie and her husband were still together. Whether the fact that they had two more children after this episode counts as a 'success' remains a moot point. It is a story which has to be told because society cannot absolve itself from responsibility.

There is, perhaps, no better breeding ground for human misery than the home where Jessie's life began. Again, if we were not so careless about those who exert an influence on the formative years of our children, Jessie might have had a totally different outlook on life.

I remember the way she stood in front of the doctor for her final medical examination before going on to her next school. Only eleven years of age at the time, her overdeveloped breasts gave her the appearance of a thirteen-year-old.

Her mother, who sat beside her, wore a sullen expression which was echoed on the child's face when the doctor said quietly, 'I think she ought to have exercises... her posture is very poor.'

'I don't 'old with doctors,' answered her mother brazenly.

Doctor and I ignored her polemics. Not even the vestige of a smile crossed the doctor's face, although I had to hide a smile by turning over the leaves of the care committee dossier on this family. The record of my predecessor's visits made it abundantly clear that she had been unable to make any headway in this home. Jessie's parents were wholly uncooperative, both with regard to Jessie and her younger sister Mildred, who was in all ways better looking.

Looking up again from my papers, I caught sight of the expression on the headmistress's face. Her faded blue eyes were riveted on Jessie's bosom. Mrs Jackson had been headmistress of the junior girls' department for many years and I had been fighting an instinctive dislike of her during the few months I had been honorary secretary of the school.

Fingering the silly curl dangling on her earlobe, Mrs Jackson began to scribble a note. She pushed it across the table to me. It read: 'Remind me to tell you something later.'

I made a mental note not to bother. In the few months I had known Mrs Jackson, I had learned that all her stories, somehow or other, had a flavour of sex. Her short, unsatisfactory marriage in the distant past, had clearly left her sublimating her emotions by the authority she wielded over two hundred little girls aged between seven and eleven. The monitress she would select to run her errands would invariably be chosen for her prettiness.

That was when I noticed that Jessie's sister Mildred was quite pretty. Conversely, the child for whom she did not care would be as plain as Jessie, unless she were... like Jessie... sufficiently well developed to capture her attention. How much, I wondered at the time, did Jessie understand about all this?

I watched Mrs Jackson's eyes follow Jessie's ungainly figure as the child walked behind the screen to dress. In a rasping voice she addressed Jessie's mother who was following her daughter.

'I'm glad to see her underwear is clean today, Mrs Carter,' she said with curled lips, 'her knickers were filthy yesterday. That'll do...' she added quickly before the angry mother could protest, '...Doctor is waiting for the next child.'

A pretty little girl, also bare to the waist, was moving into position with her mother near the doctor. Mrs Jackson fawned upon her and the child looked coy.

I glanced at the doctor, wondering what her reaction, if any, was to it all, but found her absorbed in the work of completing Jessie's medical history, ready to be passed on to the next school. I wondered how Mrs Jackson had come to know that Jessie's knickers had been dirty the day before. I was quite sure her class didn't have PT on Wednesdays.

Apart from a strange story of masochism, in which Jessie was involved, and which had no sequel worth recording, because it turned out to be nothing but a group of children finding a way to avoid going to school, the three years which Jessie subsequently spent at the big girls' school passed without incident according to the voluntary social worker of the school with whom I remained in contact, because I knew that Jessie's younger sister would eventually follow her into that school.

I heard no more of Jessie or Mildred until a good many years later when two grubby little children named Brett, newcomers to the nursery department at Mavenna Street School, made it necessary for me to visit their mother who had been neglecting their medical needs. Although there was something vaguely familiar about Mrs Brett, I didn't connect her with the Jessie Carter I had known. When admitted to the home, I found not only the two grubby children gambolling on the floor, but a baby whining in a cot. The kitchen was very untidy but it had been recently redecorated a gaudy, pillar-box red. Here and there, bold dashes of bright yellow offended the eye. It was airless and smelly.

I felt the need to gain the confidence of this sullen-faced woman who plumped down opposite me.

'Who did the decorating?' I asked ingenuously.

'Me 'ubby,' she replied, giving it a full sweeping glance, "e's dollin' up the ole place... we got the two top floors, y'know.' She was clearly proud of their extensive accommodation. She tucked her skirt more tightly under her knees to hide a large tear.

'Doesn't your husband think you should take Carol to the clinic regularly?' I said, moving on to the purpose of my visit and giving her an opportunity to blame her husband.

"E's a shift worker,' she said, on the defensive, 'it's very okkerd. Mind you, we 'as a motorcycle combination and 'e takes me w'en 'e can.'

'But you don't have to wait until he takes you,' I suggested, 'the clinic's not that far away that you can't walk there with the children. You could push the baby along in the pram.'

Some inadequate excuses followed. I felt it had something to do with the motorcycle, but her whole demeanour was evasive and I made little headway. Eventually I succeeded in persuading her to keep the next appointment. She preceded me down the narrow stairs on my way out. Near the bottom, she tripped and fell down the few remaining stairs into the hall. Before she picked herself up and adjusted her torn skirt, which was probably the cause of her fall, I saw that she had nothing on underneath.

'Those poor kids,' I said to myself, as I walked down the road. I did not realise what I had stumbled upon that afternoon until the storm broke several weeks later.

★

Although it was scarcely a month since I had visited her in her kitchen, I doubt whether I would have recognised Mrs Brett the next time I saw her if little Carol hadn't rushed to greet her at the school gates. One side of her face was so swollen that the eye was buried in a mass of blue-black flesh while the rest of her face was covered in yellow-green bruises. She was entirely without make-up, not even on her thick, shapeless mouth. It would have been pointless for me to ask any questions. There were too many mothers hovering at the exit gates anyway, collecting their children from the nursery department, so I returned to the school building and telephoned the divisional treatment organiser at the clinic.

'I need an excuse', I told her, 'to visit Mrs Brett. Did she keep the last appointment I made for Carol?'

She had, but the organiser provided me with an adequate excuse for calling on Mrs Brett again. Apparently she had forgotten to bring the daily record chart which she was supposed to keep to show the doctor at the clinic.

'You have to have that chart tomorrow, mustn't you?' I persuaded the organiser.

'Well…' she began.

'Of course you must!' I told her. 'Now don't you let me down if she does turn up with it, will you?' She laughed cooperatively.

Mrs Brett herself opened the front door to me. Standing behind her, apparently eager to know who it was, was a young girl whom I recognised immediately.

'Aren't you Mildred Carter?' I said.

The girl smiled.

'How's school?' I asked her.

'Fine,' she replied, 'have you come to see my mum?'

I shook my head. 'I've come to see Mrs Brett,' I told her, watching the back of Mrs Brett mounting the stairs.

Mildred gave the back of the retreating woman a contemptuous stare before slipping back into the front room on the ground floor. I followed Mrs Brett up the stairs.

Inside the gaudy kitchen, Mrs Brett said, 'I'm not friends with me sister any more...'

I must have looked extremely foolish as Mrs Brett went into a fit of giggles which was thoroughly incongruous with that bruised face.

'Jessie Carter!' I exclaimed.

She nodded. 'I thought you didn't recognise me,' she said. Her face had regained its sullenest.

'For heaven's sake, Jessie, how old are you?' I exclaimed, completely taken aback, my eyes lingering on the children. 'Why did you quarrel with your mother and Mildred?' I went on, not waiting for the answer to my first question.

'That woman downstairs ain't my mother. She's my stepmother. We don't 'ave nuthin' to do with 'er. Nor me sister.'

'And your father?'

'Dead. Dropped dead a coupla years ago. Good riddance too, I 'ated 'im.'

'Is Mildred happy with her stepmother?'

'Dunno. 'Spect so.' She shrugged her shoulders indifferently.

'Tell me what happened,' I said, 'it's so long since I saw you.'

'Me father married again. Six months after me mum died. 'E wuz a terrible one for drink, 'e wuz. Used to knock me abaht after me mum died. Then 'e married that one downstairs.' She made a disdainful thumb movement to indicate the downstairs home and I registered a mental note to enquire whether the district moral welfare officer was aware of Mildred's domestic set-up.

'Was that why you married so young?' I asked her.

She didn't answer for a moment.

'Nah,' she said at length, 'we wuz goin' steady anyway. Tony's ma was sorry for me too.'

'Did you *have* to marry?' I enquired.

In recent years, such a question to a teenager seemed to be taken as a compliment, the ability to answer in the positive becoming almost a matter of pride.

She nodded with alacrity, 'Tony wuzn't seventeen until we wuz married three months,' she volunteered.

'Hm,' I murmured, thinking aloud, 'three little ones already. What does Tony do?'

'Engineer,' she replied.

It was a title covering a variety of occupations in that neighbourhood, and I didn't seek clarification. She was keeping an eye on the door behind me as though she expected someone to come in. I unburdened myself of the excuse for my visit but I felt that she wasn't really listening.

'How did you get that injury to your face?' I asked, interrupting myself.

'Fell over the 'oover me 'ubby bought me for a present.' It came out much too slickly.

'All those injuries from falling over a Hoover!' I exclaimed. 'You do seem to do a lot of falling, Jessie! You fell down the stairs last time I was here.'

She nodded.

'You're not telling me the truth,' I told her. 'Tony did it, didn't he? He knocks you about, doesn't he?' I was fuming at the thought.

'It's all right now,' she stuttered defensively.

I had knocked her off her guard by the directness of my question.

I was about to follow it up when she said, 'I 'ad it cummin' to me.'

'Why is Tony knocking you about?' I asked her, trying to stifle the anger in my voice.

She shifted from one foot to the other.

'Come on,' I encouraged her, 'tell me why he beat you.'

With her bruised eyes on the door behind me, she repeated, 'I 'ad it cummin' to me. It's orl right now,' she said stubbornly, 'I 'ad it cummin' to me.'

We had reached an impasse and I rose to go. 'Please bring Carol's chart to the clinic tomorrow,' I reminded her, 'the specialist wants to see it. It's very important.'

She agreed to do so and I turned the knob of the kitchen door.

'Oos in the kitchen?' said a man's voice from the landing above.

'It's the welfare lady from the school,' answered Jessie in a submissive voice behind me.

The young man peered down at me as I emerged from the kitchen, favouring me with an insolent stare. He wore tight black jeans and his coarsely checked, open-necked shirt was tucked into the band around his slim waist. A straight fair lock of hair hung heavily over his brow in the fashion of the latest teenage rock and roll singer. He still managed to look quite handsome.

'Mr Brett,' I said, moving up one stair at a time. Experience had taught me to hold my ground and I intended to show him that I was not intimidated by him. 'I just called about Carol's medical chart. Your wife has to bring it to the clinic tomorrow,' I continued, mounting yet another stair, 'but I'm really very anxious about your wife as well. She seems to be badly injured. I knew Jessie when she attended Mavenna Street School, you know...'

I had very nearly reached him. He looked at me closely. Then he pushed open the door from which, no doubt, he had just emerged.

'Cummin,' he said and, looking down at Jessie he shouted, 'make some char, you!'

I went into the room ahead of him because he stood aside to let me pass. He leaned against the door, closing it with his back.

'Have a seat, madam,' he said in a somewhat affected voice.

For a moment I didn't know what to say or think. I was staring at the very latest radiant heat gas fire which was sending out a cosy warmth to a small room. The whole room was as completely out of place in that particular house as their red and yellow kitchen would have been in a palace. The door against which this loose-limbed boy leaned was convex and was upholstered in quilted white plastic. The sofa on which I found myself was also covered in quilted white plastic, as was the convex fireplace surround framing that elegant gas fire. Facing me stood the very latest design in cocktail cabinets in bleached wood, its door thrown open to exhibit crystal glass reflected in a bevelled mirror.

Tony switched off the wireless which seemed to be part of this extravagant drinks cabinet. I began to collect my scattered wits as I looked down on the two luxurious, thick, white lambskin rugs slung carelessly over black carpeting. The situation was about as unreal as anything I'd ever come across in all the years I had spent in this down-to-earth neighbourhood.

I turned my head to look out of the window in an effort to compose myself. Through that window I saw, on the opposite side of the road, the row of mean little houses, all replicas of the one I was in. My eyes took in the heavy black and white folkweave curtains on the windows of the room.

They were tastefully flashed with a lively red, which matched the bright red scatter cushions on the sofa and armchairs. My mind was beginning to formulate a question when Jessie appeared with two cups of tea on a tray. Without uttering a word, she laid the tray on the shiny black table in front of her husband.

'Where's the sugar?' he bellowed.

'In the cups,' she answered meekly, her eyes downcast.

I waited until she had closed the door behind her.

'Tony,' I began, 'I know you won't mind me calling you Tony, after all, you're only about twenty. Why did you make such a brutal attack on Jessie? The law doesn't—'

'Don't you come the lawr on me,' he interrupted, 'I know all about the lawr,' he added scornfully.

'Then you must know', I told him crisply, 'that it will not permit you to beat your wife.'

He picked up one of the cups by its handle, ignored the saucer and clasped its bowl with his other hand.

'*She* won't bring the lawr on me,' he replied. 'She knows she 'ad it cummin' to 'er. She knows wot she'll get if she tries to cover it up with paint,' he went on, 'you arsk 'er. Go on,' he goaded me, 'you arsk 'er yerself!' He crashed the cup down angrily on its saucer.

'Cummere,' he shouted. 'Jessie, d'ye 'ear me, cummere!'

She was standing in the doorway, a strange contrast to her young husband who clearly took care over his appearance. A large safety pin anchored the belt of her tight crumpled skirt. The side fastening no longer worked, and a soiled slip was visible in the gaping slit. No corset restricted in any way the rotundity of her stomach and the torn creased blouse which covered her unrestrained bosom was bundled thickly into her clumsy waistline. Unbrushed hair hung limply down the sides of her bruised face.

'Tell the welfare lady why I 'it ye,' Tony shouted, 'go on, tell 'er!'

Jessie began to snivel. 'Oh, Tony,' she whimpered.

'Bah!' he spat at her. 'I ain't goin' to let 'er go away thinkin'—'

'Sit down, Jessie,' I interrupted him quietly.

Jessie looked at her husband.

'You 'eard,' he said.

She sat diffidently on the edge of one of the white upholstered upright chairs.

'I told yer,' she said to me between sobs, her heavy mouth trembling piteously, 'it's orl right now. It's my fault. It won't 'appen no more.'

'Stop beating about the bush, both of you,' I said a trifle impatiently, 'what won't happen any more?'

'Go on,' shouted Tony, 'you lousy stinkin' pro, you tell 'er! Makes me want to throw up wen I look at yer!'

'Jessie,' I said, turning to her, 'do you mean to say that, with three little ones to look after… and this lovely home… you were playing the fool?'

Tony's eyes flashed. 'What did I tell yer?' he bellowed. 'But I make 'er work now I do! Same as I 'ave to do. Twelve and fifteen hours a day, I bin workin'. Overtime an' all, to buy this fer 'er.'

With an impressive gesture which took in all the affluence of their surroundings, he continued, 'Motorcycle combination I bought too, so's we could 'ave days in the country, so's she could show off. That ain't good enough for 'er! Oh no! Car, *she* 'as to 'ave to muck abaht in. In front o' me kids too. 'Ow d'ye like that! The lousy whore!'

His eyes were blazing. 'The lawr,' he snorted at me, 'don't you try to tell me abaht the lawr! Wot kinda lawr is it that says a woman like that can 'ave me kids an' I carn't!'

The tears were now rolling down the bruised, tormented ugliness that was Jessie's face. She was blinking through them at the quivering anger of her boy husband.

'I told yer it wouldn't 'appen no more, Tony. Yer promised.' Her voice trailed off to a whisper. 'Yer said I—'

'Yeh,' he interrupted, 'but I ain't goin' to let this 'ere welfare woman think...'

'Sit down, Tony,' I said in my most authoritative voice, trying hard to take command of the situation. His accusing finger dropped to his side.

'Stop behaving like a bully,' I said, raising my voice, 'I've known Jessie since she was a little girl. The only lie she told me today is that she got all those facial injuries from falling over the Hoover *you* gave her as a present.'

A little of the overbearing arrogance seemed to leave him. He flung himself into the armchair and picked up his cup again.

'What has the law to do with all this?' I asked, lowering my voice again.

'I've spent a lot o' time and money on the law,' Tony said bitterly. 'We 'ad nuthin' but bare boards wen we wuz married. I worked 'ard, I did, fer all this. It ain't all paid for neither an' wot does she do wen me back is turned? Wotcher think *she* gets up to? An' with an ole cow like Sarah Blake. Sixty, if she's a day. Motorcycle combination ain't good for 'er lydyship, Jessie. Oh no,' he snorted angrily, 'the ole cow 'as a *car* if yer please and this 'ere pro don't mind messing abaht with 'er in the car. In front of me kids, too!'

'Are the children all safe in the kitchen alone?' I asked, suddenly remembering them.

'Go an' see to your kids,' he ordered Jessie, who rose obediently. When she had gone, he went on, his voice full of self-pity. 'I've been to the personnel manager where I work. 'E told me to leave 'er. So did the man I saw at the court. So I went to a solicitor. 'E wrote me a letter. I got it 'ere.' He fished out a letter from the back pocket of his jeans. 'Because I let 'er stay 'ere, 'E sez I condoned it all. 'E don't think I'll get me kids.' He spread the letter out before me.

'Condoned means—' Tony was about to explain to me but I interrupted him by crossing to the door and opening it.

'Jessie,' I called, 'if the children are safe, come back in here. Why aren't you at work?' I asked Tony, listening for Jessie's footsteps.

'It ain't my shift. Anyway, I feel like throwin' in me job. Let 'em take the furniture away. I don't care no more.'

Jessie was whimpering in the doorway. 'Tony, ye promised.'

'What did he promise, Jessie?' I asked.

Between sobs she explained. He had agreed that so long as she did everything he ordered her to do, she could stay.

I felt suddenly very sorry for Jessie.

'Are you so very fond of this old woman?' I asked Jessie, trying to wither Tony with a baleful stare.

Jessie shook her head miserably.

'She don't 'ave to like 'er,' supplied Tony scathingly, 'to do what she does! Standing naked she wuz. The bloody whore. In this room w'en I come in. An' that dirty old cow wuz sittin' in my armchair!' His words were full of anger. 'Makin' a bloody fool of me in front of the neighbours. I bet 'er sister told 'em all, the little bitch! I took Jessie away from 'er father, I did, because 'e wuz beatin' the livin' daylights out o' 'er. Wot a bloody fool I wuz! Mildred's right. I should've let 'im break 'er bleedin' neck!'

'Are you quite sure it's all Jessie's fault?' I found myself asking Tony, so quietly that I felt them both staring at me in surprise.

'Wotcher mean?' exclaimed Tony in aggrieved tones.

'I'm not at all sure', I replied, 'that you aren't in some way to blame for all this. However that may be, there is no justification for the injuries you have inflicted on Jessie.

Some of her bruises are more recent than others, which lead me to think they weren't all inflicted at the same time. You've taken to hitting her whenever you feel like it, haven't you?'

He didn't reply. She didn't speak either. She was crying silently now.

'Answer me, Jessie,' I said sharply. 'Isn't that right?'

She nodded.

'I'll teach 'er,' he threatened vehemently. 'Why don't she go and live with that ole cow?' He sneered at Jessie. 'Why don't yer go where yer wanted? It don't make 'er sick to look at yer.'

'Oh, Tony,' she wept, 'yer said I could stay. I told yer I love ye.'

'Bah!' spat her young husband, 'yer wudden give up all this, woodya, for 'er bits o' sticks.' He took in the whole theatrical decor with a sweep of his hands.

'I don't want to leave yer,' sobbed Jessie. 'I told yer it won't never 'appen again. Yer said I could stay. Oh, Tony,' Jessie whispered.

'Now listen to me, Tony,' I began with some impatience, 'you know from the solicitor that, having condoned Jessie's behaviour, you must either make the best of things or get out of here yourself.' I wasn't entirely sure that Jessie knew why he had agreed to her staying in the house, but it was worth a try to give her some bargaining power.

'You'd like me to go, wudden ya, so's ye could 'ave all this,' he howled at Jessie.

'No, Tony,' she wailed, 'I told yer I woodent,' she wailed.

'I want you both to understand,' I went on, 'please listen to me for a moment, because all this,' I indicated their belongings, 'is so terribly important to both of you, you forget that there is far more to a happy life than straining for more and more possessions. Jessie had a miserable childhood. She may think she wants all this to make her happy but she needs, more than anything else, to feel wanted.' I turned to face Tony.

'Are you really being honest with yourself', I asked him, 'when you say you were buying all this for Jessie? You wanted it for yourself, didn't you? It makes you feel big, doesn't it?'

He didn't answer.

'I think you've both made a thorough mess of things,' I continued quickly in order not to lose the momentum, 'and now you've brought three helpless little beings into the world. Do you want those kids to end up in care, or worse, listening to you both screaming at each other?' I looked steadily at Tony. 'If you break up your marriage now, you will be offering the same insecurity to them that Jessie had throughout her miserable childhood.'

There was no reply from either of them, nor any indication whether I was making any headway with Tony.

I was trying hard to think of something more to say. My job was to care for children, I was telling myself mentally. As far as I was concerned they could mess their own lives up as much as they wanted to do. I was concerned with the welfare of those three little children they had been careless enough to bring into their unhappy home. Marriage guidance was definitely *not* my function, I told myself.

And then it struck me! I was actually making up my mind to hand the whole sorry story to the moral welfare department at County Hall when the idea came to me, which is why I believe that the story of Jessie is, at least, one of my 'partial successes'.

I kept my eyes on Tony and injected as much authority into my voice as I could muster.

'Listen to me carefully, Tony,' I said, 'I would like to make an appointment for you both to see a very nice man, a marriage guidance counsellor. He's used to hearing stories like yours. Is there anyone who would mind the children when you keep the appointment?'

Neither answered.

'Come on, Tony,' I coaxed, 'answer me. You really have only three possible ways out of this predicament. You can leave Jessie. The children will, of course, remain with her. You don't want that, you say. That leaves two other possibilities. You can go on beating Jessie until the law intervenes. If you do much more of that *I'll* soon see that the law steps in to punish you for being such a bully. And,' I hesitated momentarily, just for effect, 'there is the third choice I've just mentioned. You can talk all this over with that nice man I mentioned a moment ago. He could help you both to mend your marriage. You told me, Tony, that you want to keep your children. Well, here's your chance to give them a better life than Jessie ever had. Answer me! Is there someone who would care for the children if I make this appointment?'

'Tony's mum would,' said Jessie, the gleam of hope showing on her tearful face.

'Answer me, Tony,' I said sharply. 'What are you going to do? Are you going to give your little ones a better chance in life than Jessie ever had?'

He was standing with his back to the elegant fireplace, legs apart, staring at the ceiling. He reminded me of a fighting turkey cock. The arrogance of his stance angered me. I glanced at Jessie. She returned my look with a pathetic, watery hopefulness.

'I want an answer, Tony,' I said firmly. 'If you weren't really fond of Jessie, deep down inside, you would have left her and you know it. She has hurt you very badly. Your pride has been badly affected. But I doubt whether either of you understands what it is all about. Do I make that appointment?'

I stared him straight in the eyes, hoping I sounded more sure of myself than I felt.

'Yeah. All right,' he agreed at last, reluctantly. It had taken him a minute or so to answer and I thought I had lost the battle. 'What's there to lose anyway that ain't lost...?' he added as an afterthought.

'Now,' I said, hiding my relief, 'you'll arrange with your mother to look after the children?'

'Yeah,' he said, which was the most conciliatory remark he had made so far.

It was plainly time for me to go.

He transferred his stare to Jessie. 'Show the lady down,' he commanded her, half-ashamed of his acquiescence.

Jessie got up from the chair humbly. I shook his hand and followed her down the stairs. Looking at her overdeveloped figure, the scene in the medical room, so many years before, floated before my eyes. The child, self-conscious of her large breasts, the head teacher, Mrs Jackson, who could have warped so many young minds before the scandal which resulted in her premature retirement. Had Jessie been one of her victims?

Mrs Jackson's face came before my mind's eye, those silly curls dangling beside her ears. I was hugging myself for having avoided passing the problem of the Brett family to that special unit at County Hall which dealt with sexual problems. I was banking on that marriage guidance counsellor. There was so much prejudice at that time against homosexuals. Somehow I didn't think Jessie was a lesbian. I really did believe she was fond of her husband. She might be bisexual, of course, I was telling myself as I bade her goodbye. Her answer to the final question I put to her on the doorstep encouraged me to think otherwise.

I whispered, 'Tell me, Jessie, why did you do such a thing to Tony?'

The significance of her choked reply was as sad as anything I've ever encountered among the children whose troubles had been my preoccupation for so many years.

'Old Sarah made me feel like I wuz somebody,' she said.

Monkey Business

From the back, it looked like a little monkey. Straggly hair jutted out from behind the baldish pate like sparse grass. I caught up with it and was horrified to discover that it was a monkey in front as well... a poor, wizened little monkey with a white face. All the movements were as awkward as those of a chimpanzee.

'What's your name?' I asked, expecting it to chatter.

'Pennyloap,' was the swift reply, from lips that were as mobile as a monkey's. Its eyes also darted to and fro, monkey fashion.

I stood with my back to the lamp-post, in case it suddenly decided to swing up it, but it made no attempt to escape.

I began to walk alongside the little monkey, wondering how long it would be before it led me to the place from which it had escaped. It was dressed in the weirdest clothes. Everything was too big, and there was far too much of it. Most of the items adhered by means of large safety pins.

'How old are you, Penelope?' I asked ingratiatingly, remembering just in time to rhyme the name with 'pope'.

'Seven,' she said.

'Where do you live?'

'Forest Lane.'

I blinked. I knew the street, and the address seemed appropriate.

We walked in silence.

'Do you go to school?' I asked, trying to prolong the conversation.

'No, don't want to,' she replied shortly.

'Any brothers or sisters?' I went on.

'Yes,' she answered. 'Two brothers. They goes to Mavenna Street School, but I won't go there!'

'Why?' I asked cautiously.

'Don't want to!' she repeated.

'Doesn't your mum want you to?'

'She do, but me dad don't!'

'Why?' I asked again.

'He says they don't larn you nuthin' that do any good!'

I professed to be gravely interested. 'But what are you "larnin" here?' I asked.

'Plenty!'

It was clear that we had reached a dead end. I tried again. 'Tell me about your brothers...'

'There's Bill and Jim,' said the little monkey, 'and me. *They* don't like me... *I'm* the favourite,' she added quickly.

Did she add that too quickly, I wondered?

'Bill and Jim who?' I said, with pretended indifference.

'Thomas, of course,' she said contemptuously.

We had reached Mavenna Street. She took one look at the place she was in and was about to dart off.

'Wait a minute,' I said, 'shake hands!'

We shook hands solemnly, and she was gone. The handshake, it occurred to me afterwards, assured me that she was real.

I hurried to the school, climbed half a dozen staircases, in which exercise I was by now well trained, and finally reached the medical room, rather breathless. The school nurse was there.

'I've seen a little missing link!' I said.

Sister went on calmly rolling bandages.

'Do you hear, Sister?' I insisted, 'I've just had a long conversation with a monkey. It lives in this neighbourhood, it's seven years of age, it doesn't go to school, and it isn't going to go either!'

There was no immediate reply from the nurse. Evidently she was determined to keep this outward calm, no matter what startling news I brought.

'There are several "monkeys" in this neighbourhood,' she said at last, 'now which one would you be talking about?'

There were moments when this particular nurse, who left shortly after I became the school's honorary secretary, sorely tried me. This was one of those moments. It is their training which makes them accept voluntary workers, and their enthusiastic approach to human problems, with exaggerated calm.

Icily, I repeated my news.

'Indeed,' said Sister, 'and where does it live?'

'Forest Lane.'

'Impossible,' she replied, 'that's not my beat, but I know all the children there.'

I smiled patronisingly. 'It's a Thomas!'

'I'm sure I know the Thomases,' said Sister, puzzled, 'and they haven't got a monkey... their two boys, Bill and Jim are in the school, aren't they?'

'S'right,' I said calmly, '*and* there's Peneloap!'

'There's who?'

'Peneloap,' I said with satisfaction. 'I've just made her acquaintance. Shows that you don't know everything,' I added, trying to annoy her.

'What are you going to do about Peneloap?' she asked, after a pause, doing me the favour of making it rhyme with 'pope' too.

'Discover what it is all about and get it into school,' I said, 'that should humanise her.'

'It should,' said Sister dryly.

*

The school attendance officer also didn't believe me.

'All right,' I told him, 'go and see for yourself!' And, within a month, the little animal was at school.

*

They came, almost from far and wide, to see it.

We arranged for its first medical examination, and summoned the mother to attend.

She came, and wept copiously throughout the examination. No wonder, perhaps, for when we had extracted the little monkey from her wrappings it was the most ill-nourished little creature I'd ever seen. She had obviously been all clothes.

Doctor was very gentle and tried everything to persuade the mother, but she was adamant. Her child was *not* going to have any medical attention, if she could help it. I followed the doctor's sign language, and we let the mother go.

'Where do we go from here?' said Sister, breathing out, as she closed the door behind the queer couple. She looked at me with a glint in her eye which was unmistakable.

'She's all yours,' she added, 'you found her, now you deal with her!'

The doctor laughed. 'All yours!' she said, and I thanked them both ironically.

★

On the following day I knocked at the door of 23 Forest Lane. Mrs Thomas appeared with a grin on her face, her two front teeth spearing me.

'May I come in?'

'Whoffer?' she asked suspiciously.

'I don't know,' I said truthfully, 'except that I'd like to talk to you.'

We entered a room in which were masses of filthy rags.

'Does your husband work?' I asked, making conversation.

'He's a rag dealer,' she replied. 'We keep all the rags here.' She indicated the evil-smelling heaps.

'Where do you all live?' I enquired.

'Whatya want to know for?'

'Because I want to help you, Mrs Thomas,' I replied. 'Like all of us, you have your troubles.'

That seemed to allay suspicion. She led me to a back room. A started bottle of milk stood on the dirty table. The door of a cupboard was open and inside were many more started bottles of milk, lumps of stale bread, half-finished pots of jam with knives sticking out of them, and open packets of sugar.

A mouse scuttled across the floor. I can take monkeys, but not mice. I nearly took to my heels. Steadying my nerves, I began.

'Peneloap is a very sick child, Mrs Thomas. Won't you let us help her?'

'No!' she said firmly.

'Why?' I asked.

'Her dad'll kill me... he'd leave me... he loves Peneloap... he loves the woman next door, too, but,' she added craftily, 'he'll never leave me while there's Peneloap.'

Poor little Penelope, I thought, and wondered how much of this was true. If her husband was as crafty as Mrs Thomas, I was up against it.

'When can I see Mr Thomas?' I asked, without relish.

'He'll be 'ere in a minit,' she replied and, indeed, not much later he came lumbering in.

Primitive and with a low cunning, I surmised, physically powerful and, no doubt, formidable when angered.

I beamed at him, feeling far from cheerful, and annoyed with myself for my lack of courage.

'Mr Thomas,' I began, 'your little girl is now at school and she is getting on fine. But she's very delicate and we'd like to send her to hospital for a good check-up…'

'Yer won't,' he growled, eyeing me as if measuring the size of his adversary.

'Well, of course, if you'd rather she died…' I said meaningfully, with an eye on the exit, inwardly petrified.

'Died?' he shouted.

'Yes!' I lied.

'My Peneloap ain't gonna die!' he said angrily.

'Of course not,' I soothed, 'if she has medical attention, she'll be all right.'

His small eyes narrowed even more and he looked calculating.

'What's wrong with 'er?' He waved an arm towards the half-empty milk bottle, the started packets of sugar and the rest of the decaying foodstuffs. 'My ole woman gives a pound a week to the milkman.'

Not certain which one of the parents was at fault, I decided to play safe.

'I'm sure your wife's doing her best, Mr Thomas,' I said, 'but she's not a doctor. Your little Peneloap is ill. Now do let me have your consent', I coaxed, 'to a really good check-up…'

'How long will they keep her?' he demanded, eyeing me again.

'A week, maybe two,' I replied, endeavouring to make it sound like an hour.

He brooded. 'One week,' he said loudly, raising his arm as if to strike his wife, 'and then I want 'er back! D'ye 'ear!' He bellowed his last remark at Mrs Thomas and went out.

I jumped as the mouse scuttled past my feet once more.

'Thank you, Mrs Thomas,' I said, rapidly emerging with relief into the fresh air.

Back at school, I checked the boys' medical cards. Both were moderately healthy and mentally normal. Strange. Neither parent, by ordinary standards, was. Strange, also, that the little monkey herself seemed very clever.

It took weeks of research. I discovered that Mrs Thomas's elderly parents lived a few streets away, were an eminently respectable, decent, hard-working old couple, who continually helped their daughter financially and 'covered up' for her in every way, admitting her shortcomings not even to themselves.

I managed to discover, also, the cause of the sparse hair. Every time Mrs Thomas became emotionally involved, she tugged out a lump. Every time the boys quarrelled with Penelope – and this happened frequently – they did the same. It was rapidly becoming apparent that, if this process continued, we should have a completely bald child on our hands. There was little I could do about the matter, except bribe the boys to leave the little girl's hair alone and administer veiled threats to Mrs Thomas by oblique references to the 'cruelty man'.

The mystery, however, remained. Had Penelope been deliberately underfed and neglected? And if so, who was to blame, both parents, or just one or the other? If not, why was she, unlike her brothers, undernourished? Was she, in fact, the father's favourite, or was that a child's own make-believe? Or was it said, by both mother and child, under the father's threats, in order to deceive me?

Eventually Penelope was admitted to a children's ward in a local hospital. After four days, she was home again. Mrs Thomas arrived, behaved like a wounded animal, and had forcibly grasped the almost naked monkey from the hospital bed. Nothing the doctors or the nurses could say would convince her that the child would be better left where she was. I was more puzzled than before.

Somehow, however, Penelope thrived. She developed human traits at school through her constant contact with other children. And gradually it became apparent that, by some means, that clever child had gained the whip hand in her home.

Various social organisations made attempts to rehabilitate the family – unsuccessfully. A scheme under which a social worker took over the running of the home failed. It worked happily only when she was physically present. A scheme whereby Mrs Thomas and Penelope were bodily transported to a mother and child home, there to learn the rudiments of growing up together, failed miserably. Within a week, they were back home. Seemingly, Mrs Thomas was too afraid she would find that Mr Thomas had decamped.

Still Penelope thrived and, in the end, emerged wholly victorious.

She was no longer a monkey. She had become, I thought, a vixen. Her hair, no longer sparse, was held in check by a hairnet. Only her eyes still darted hither and thither in that unmistakable monkey-like fashion. Her two brothers had departed from the family abode and her ageing, and ailing, parents spent their days and nights quarrelling. The old couple could be seen any summer's day, sitting on rickety chairs outside their smelly home. Now and then Penelope rewarded them with a half-pint of bitter. The home itself, although it smelt, was comparatively clean. Penelope seemed to keep herself, and them, on National Assistance and her parents' old age pensions.

Some social workers were greatly concerned as to the fate of Penelope when her parents were finally laid to rest. Untrained for any vocation, other than that of managing her parents, they felt that nothing but harm would befall her.

I myself took another view. Penelope was now no longer a child. I couldn't 'love' her even when she was. I found her positively repulsive and I didn't trust her. In fact, my instincts proved to be right.

She knew that one day, those parents of hers would cease to mount guard over her home. I was certain, unpleasant though the thought was, that she was secretly waiting for the moment of release.

She thought I didn't know, although some of her neighbours were good friends of mine, that she was quietly carrying on the family business with considerable skill and making a tidy profit.

I left that area of social work convinced that one day someone would marry – or murder – Penelope for the money which she was slowly amassing behind that façade of a dutiful daughter. And, in the meantime, she had us all exactly where she wanted us.

Sensibility

One winter's day I found myself needing to make a really urgent visit. Freddy and Ernie Black, their form masters told me, were becoming literally impossible at school. None of the children would sit beside them.

Children do not mince words. Casually, I questioned many of the boys of both classes, when I could get them to myself, and they all told me point-blank that the two brothers 'smelt' or 'smelt sumfink orful'. The teachers admitted being forced to segregate them from the rest of their classmates.

One's first encounter with such a situation has, perhaps, an element of the ridiculous. It is not difficult to conceive, however, the effect of segregation on the minds of these two small boys who had neither the chance to select their home, nor the opportunity to choose their mother.

I knew that incontinence was a common childhood ailment and that it is almost always possible to cure, but, so far as Mrs Black was concerned, nothing could be done for her boys because she would not, or could not, attend their medical examinations at school. The cards which I sent to her remained unanswered, or had the words 'going to own doctor' scribbled on them.

The visit could be delayed no longer, although the prospect did not appeal to me. I imagined that I was likely to find myself in one of the dirtiest homes in the neighbourhood.

It was, therefore, a pleasant surprise to find my knock answered by a plump, motherly woman who opened the door and invited me in wholeheartedly. There was a roaring fire in the kitchen sitting room, blocked from sight, however, by a clothes horse which was covered with nether garments of various shapes, sizes and descriptions. They were all dripping merrily away on the stone floor, which was scrupulously clean.

Mrs Black pretended not to see my stare.

'I'm the school voluntary worker, Mrs Black,' I said, 'and I should be glad to have your consent to send the boys to the enuresis clinic.' I explained the meaning of the word.

She was standing with her back to the door, looking at me, but avoiding my gaze.

'They won't go, Doctor,' she replied.

'I'm not a doctor, Mrs Black,' I said, 'but they really are in need of treatment. It is the school doctor who asked me to call.'

'They won't go,' she repeated.

'That's very unusual,' I said. 'Why is that?'

She didn't reply.

'Mrs Black,' I persisted, 'you surely don't allow a ten-year-old child and one of eight to tell you what they'll do?'

'It's no good, Nurse,' she replied, insisting on a title for me, 'they won't do as I ask them. I've even called the doctor to them, and they've gone out! Instead, I wash every day knickers and sheets and knickers and sheets, until I feel like screaming...'

'I can well understand your feelings,' I said, 'although I'm not a nurse. What reason do they give for not wanting to go to the clinic?'

She sighed wearily and again refused to answer. More sternness on my part seemed indicated.

'Surely you are not such a weak woman, as to let them dictate to you...?'

I was looking at her sallow, tired face, her neatly appointed home, and back to her face, as I spoke. Some odd sense, derived perhaps from constant visits to all manner of people, came to my aid. Her soft brown eyes were searching mine, as if she were reading them, and I took a chance.

'Mrs Black,' I asked, interrupting my own thoughts, 'you are not, by any chance, of the Jewish faith?'

The gentle smile, with which she had accepted my last reproof, vanished as if I had wiped it off with a cloth. What was obviously fear, a real fear, crept into her eyes.

'How did you guess?' she faltered, 'no one knows here… the children will suffer enough in this life as it is… I don't even buy the meat locally…'

'I don't know, I'm sure,' I answered, deliberately adopting the most matter-of-fact voice I could manage, 'I have a good deal to do with people hereabouts, the Baptists and the Nonconformists, the Catholics and the non-believers… the Scots,' I laughed, 'and the Welsh and the Irish.'

She was watching my face, only partly reassured, and I suppressed the emotion which rose in me. This was, I thought, only a few years after the end of the bloodiest war in history. Only a few years since the full knowledge of Hitler's inhuman crimes had reached, and echoed around, the civilised world. Only a few years since the end of the Holocaust and a world war which, among other things, had been fought for man's inalienable right to worship his God in his own way.

No right-minded man or woman could have remained unmoved by the haunted look in those soft brown eyes. Anyway, I couldn't.

'Mrs Black,' I said slowly, 'I don't care if you worship the great god Pan or the sun, the moon and the stars… I had a reason for asking you that question.'

There were suppressed tears in her eyes now.

'Come and sit down here beside me,' I said, 'I assure you I had no unkind reason.'

She moved towards me, uneasily, and still not totally sure.

'No one at school will sit beside Fred or Ernie,' I told her, 'and that must make them very unhappy. Sooner or later someone may discover, as I did, that you are Jewish. They won't say Freddy Black is ill... they'll call him by a nasty, dirty name.'

I glanced around her neat, clean kitchen.

'I know very well, of course,' I continued, 'that you are not dirty. Your home is one of the nicest I have visited but I shall not be there when some child, who scarcely knows what he is saying, calls your child abusive names.'

I stopped myself as she looked at me with mingled pain and gratitude.

'I cannot be there, Mrs Black,' I felt I had to press on, 'every time some child shouts an ugly word at one of your children. Don't you see, you *must* see to their treatment.'

She slumped into the chair beside me but still remained silent.

'Please, Mrs Black,' I pleaded, 'let me make an appointment for the boys.'

'I can't,' she answered me, as if there were no hope at all, 'it's Nina's fault!'

'Who is Nina?' I asked, surprised.

'My daughter... she's fourteen... she goes to the other school... she's the same. She's upstairs now in bed. She won't get up to go to school, and I know why!' She uttered the last words with a little more spirit, 'The bed's wet!'

'Please bring Nina down to me,' I requested.

'She won't come,' said the mother, who knew her child.

'Then I'll have to go up to her,' I said with determination.

The threat galvanised her into action.

While she was away, I surveyed the kitchen once more. Apart from the excess of dripping garments, this was a home in every sense of the word. I felt sorry for this kind-hearted, over-indulgent woman.

She wasn't long. It was no more than five minutes before Nina stood in the doorway, with a coat over her night-dress. If I had seen her in the first place, I would have been more certain about her antecedents. The contours of her features somehow told the family secret.

'Hallo, Nina!' I said brightly.

The child gazed back at me suspiciously, and did not reply. The enigmatic expression of the Madonna was in her beautiful, oval eyes.

'I know you are not at school,' I continued, believing in the direct approach, 'because you have wet your bed and you are ashamed to get out of it.'

Still she did not speak. I tried again.

'I know too that you are Jewish.'

She opened her mouth in alarm, and looked quickly at her mother.

'Oh don't worry about that,' I said carelessly, 'your secret is quite safe with me. Whether it ever does come out, or doesn't, you don't want to be called dirty or smelly, do you?'

She struck a defiant pose.

'Listen, Nina,' I said, 'don't you think we ought to trust each other? Tell me now why you won't go to the clinic to be cured.'

She turned her head towards her mother, who seemed to understand the gesture and who began to tell the pathetic story.

The school clinic was situated facing Nina's school. The enuresis session was on Tuesdays. All the children who attended could be seen entering, and Nina was hypersensitive about her complaint. She would rather have died than be seen going into that clinic on a Tuesday afternoon.

I looked at the little girl and realised the suffering she must have endured. I knew the voluntary social worker at her school very well, and that it would be a simple matter for her to rearrange things.

'Nina,' I said, 'I'm going to do you a big favour. But I want a big favour from you in return.'

She glanced at me doubtfully. Her beautiful eyes were set in black hollows, which made me fear that her physical ailment would not so rapidly respond to treatment.

'Nina,' I reiterated, trying to sound impressive, 'I am going to get an appointment for you at a clinic which is a long way from your school. No one at your school will know that you are attending. In return, will you take Freddy and Ernie with you?'

She studied me carefully.

At last, she nodded, with obvious relief on her face.

*

Freddy and Ernie were cured very quickly but it took some years to master the kidney disorder which afflicted Nina. I took every chance to look in on Mrs Black, and ruffle Nina's hair if she was about. She was, I found, as gentle as her mother.

What surprised me, one day, was finding the school nurse there. It appeared she also liked to call upon Mrs Black, and to take a cup of tea with her. She had come across Mrs Black when she took Freddy home with a damaged knee.

'I don't know what part of the country they come from,' she said to me afterwards, with such assumed innocence and artfulness that I had to smile, 'but I like that Mrs Black.'

Bless Sister, I thought, and liked her better than ever.

Turn, thou Ghost, that Way...

Judging by the shrieks from the nursery school, I knew there was fun going on. The pull was irresistible. I went in to find the little people, ranging from three to five years, having a wonderful time. Chatting with the young teacher in charge, and watching the babies at play, was always hugely entertaining, even if also time-consuming.

That day they were throwing a large balloon-like ball into the air and watching it descend, each time in a different place, accompanied by whoops of joy. It was infectious and I could not help laughing with them... until I saw the twins. They were sitting solemnly on their small stools, watching unmoved, as the rest of the children played.

'Who are they?' I asked the teacher.

'The Carey twins.'

I remembered that they had just been admitted.

'Takes a little while before new babies conform,' she told me, 'I never force the pace...'

I looked at the twins. Skinny, with large, round, dark-shadowed eyes. Pasty, colourless faces. Thin, mousy hair.

'What are their names?' I enquired.

'Peter and Paul,' she replied, without looking at them.

I wandered over to them.

'Which of you is Peter?' I said. One twin prodded the thin chest of the other. 'Which of you is Paul?' Solemnly, the other twin imitated the gesture, and prodded the chest of his neighbour.

I laughed, but they didn't even smile. 'How old are you?'

'Three!' they answered in unison.

'Where do you live?'

There was no reply.

On my way back from the nursery, I looked in on the school nurse.

'Let's have Peter and Paul Carey up for the next medical,' I suggested, 'it's a bit long to wait for the entrant medical examination.'

'Certainly,' said the accommodating nurse cheerfully and, as always, duly arranged it.

Their mother attended. She too was small, thin and pasty, with the same large dark round eyes rimmed with black circles. Stripped to the waist, the twins looked exactly like products of one of Hitler's concentration camps.

Doctor gave me a meaningful glance. She leaned towards Mrs Carey and said gently, 'They're rather underweight for their age, Mrs Carey. There's a special clinic for investigating that kind of thing. Would you like them to be examined there? I know you're not very big yourself,' she added hastily, 'and it may be hereditary. At the same time, there may also be some reason for this lack of weight.'

Mrs Carey flushed a little, but readily agreed to the investigation.

When the twins were once more fully clothed, the doctor terminated the interview.

'Mrs Lewis will come and see you', she said, indicating me, 'before the specialist at the clinic sends for the children.'

Upon that, Mrs Carey gathered up the twins, one on each hand, and departed, followed immediately by the next little patient, with its particular mother, which gave us no chance to discuss the Careys.

Having received from the clinic the official form PH, which is part of the routine prior to an appointment at the nutrition clinic, I rang the bell of 7 Gravely Street. An old woman, who shuffled to the door in her bedroom slippers, informed me that the Careys lived on the top floor. I climbed up all forty-nine stairs. I counted them, as counting them seemed to lighten the effort.

Mrs Carey was squinting at me from the top landing while I progressed up the final flight. She smiled when she recognised me.

'It's three knocks for me,' she advised me, 'I 'ope the old girl didn't grumble!'

'She didn't,' I reassured her.

I noticed that Mrs Carey had been washing something in a basin, which stood on a rickety stand on the landing. Beside the rickety stand was an old-fashioned gas cooker.

'Come in,' she said hospitably, exposing the living room with a push of the hand which she was drying at the same time. The living room was completely bare but for a deal table and some hard chairs. A miserable fire smoked in a damp grate. The mantelpiece was decorated by a row of small round tobacco tins, behind one of which I noticed the faded photograph of a good-looking young man.

The place was spotlessly clean. Indeed, it was so bare that it could not have been difficult to keep clean. We sat down together at the table.

'I'm sorry to disturb you in the middle of your work,' I began apologetically, 'but I always think it's easier to talk when the children are not about.'

She smiled her agreement.

'Mrs Carey,' I said, trying to get to the awkward business in hand, 'we have to fill in a form.'

This particular official form was a difficult one to surmount. It contained a number of extremely personal questions, which the specialist at the nutrition centre always liked to have before the children were examined.

'You needn't answer any of the questions I ask you, if you don't want to,' I went on, 'they are just a guide for the doctor. He likes to have some idea of the background of his little patients, not,' I added lightly, 'because he thinks you are starving them to death or something.'

'In fact,' I continued glibly, 'very often it is too much sugar or something like that, not too little, which is keeping their weight down.'

Mrs Carey nodded. She seemed resigned to it all and less uncomfortable than I was.

I extracted the form from my bag and filled in the name and address, as well as each member of the family as she supplied the information.

'I see your kitchen is on the landing,' I said. 'Where does the water come from?'

'I bring it up in jugs from the ground floor,' she replied without hesitation.

'And the lavatory?' I queried.

'Downstairs, in the backyard,' was her reply.

'Any bathroom?'

She smiled. 'Of course not!'

I felt rebuked.

'Do you mind showing me where the children sleep? It is really a question of ventilation,' I murmured, as I followed her across the landing into the bedroom.

It was a front room, rather larger than the back room in which we had been sitting. In it was a double bed, two single beds and... nothing else. No cupboard, no wardrobe, no floor covering, no curtains. Each bed had blankets, and beside each bed was a neatly folded pile of what looked like clothes.

There were two tightly closed windows in the room, under each of which stood a child's bed. I remained standing in the doorway.

'We can't open the windows much,' she answered my stare, 'because of the beds.'

I agreed, adding that I thought maybe a little air could be let in during the day.

She did not answer, and we retired again to the living room.

'Mrs Carey,' I reminded her, 'you needn't answer the next question, if you'd rather not. How much does your husband earn?'

She didn't hesitate. She mentioned a very low figure.

'What does he do?' I asked, without diverting my attention from the form.

There was great pride in her voice. ''E's a civil servant!'

'Indeed,' I said, looking up, 'what exactly is his work?'

''E's a park attendant,' she volunteered.

'A park attendant?' I repeated questioningly. His wages didn't suggest it. 'What does he do?'

''E picks up all the paper and things with a special stick.'

My eyes dropped back to the form.

'How much of his wages does Mr Carey give to you?' I went on.

'All of it,' she answered simply. 'Of course, I makes 'im sandwiches and I gives 'im a bit o' pocket money back each day... we're very careful livvers, ma'am. You see them tins on the mantelpiece?' She indicated the tobacco tins with a nod of her head. 'The first is the rent, the second's gas, the third's electric, the fourth's the clothing club money, the fifth's insurance, burial, y'know...' she tailed off.

I looked at the neatly arranged tins on the mantelpiece. To me, one or two tins were commonplace, but so many were most unusual.

'Mrs Carey,' I concluded, rising, 'I'm really very grateful to you for your cooperation. I wish all mothers were so helpful.'

'Tell me,' I added, moving towards the door, 'you are not, by any chance, in debt to anybody?'

'Oh no!' she replied with dignity. 'We wouldn't dream of it. My Ted and me are very careful...'

'I was sure you were not like that,' I smiled.

She looked at me and I felt that there was something more to come.

'Yes, Mrs Carey?' I said encouragingly.

A dull pink flush began to spread across her pasty face and she glanced at the mantelpiece once more.

'I don't mind telling you,' she said, a little defiantly, 'we're saving up for something. It's in the sixth tin.'

She fixed her eyes on it. So, having counted the tins, did I. My feminine curiosity was aroused.

'Yes?' I said, a little too eagerly.

'Me and my Ted are saving hard', she revealed, 'to buy a nice tombstone for my first husband. My Ted and Joe were buddies, y'see.'

Words failed me and I mumbled my goodbye.

*

Peter and Paul were plainly cases for the nutrition centre.

On my way from Mrs Carey to my next visit, I pondered over the problem, but no solution suggested itself. Expensive tombstones were commonplace enough in this area, but the extent to which these people were carrying their ambition was certainly exceptional. It was obvious enough that there was some deep and powerful reason for this systematic deprivation, but it might prove difficult to get to the bottom of it all. My mention of the nutrition centre had been received by Mrs Carey with relative composure. She knew what it meant, particularly at that time when it had not yet been rechristened 'special investigation clinic', and was not yet dealing with the ever-increasing problem of how to cut down to size the incipient Billy and Bessie Bunter. What then was the powerful hidden motive which drove this woman to continue to starve herself and her children?

I called in on the divisional organiser, who was generally able to help when I reached an impasse, and told her about the Careys.

She sat back in her chair and mused. 'It's certainly unusual,' she said, 'but, of course, it's by no means the oddest thing I've encountered hereabouts. If this woman is not managing to deceive you and she is, in fact, a simple, decent kind of person, there must be some extraordinary motive.'

'Yes,' I said, 'but what? I've speculated on all manner of things...'

'Murder, for example?' she laughed. 'They could have murdered her first husband, I suppose, and are making amends. We had two unsolved murders in the district in recent times, you may have noticed,' she added whimsically.

'No,' I said, 'I am absolutely certain that this woman is no murderess, but you've put an idea into my head. You may have something when you speak of making amends. And yet, amends for what?'

'Well, if it isn't homicide, it might be adultery. How's that for an idea?'

'Hmmm...' I speculated, 'but somehow I don't think it is that either.'

'Well, maybe the doctor at the centre can get to the bottom of it. It seems to me, however,' she added sagely, 'it might be possible to persuade her to spread the load. By any manner of reason, the deceased can't be consumed with impatience for his tombstone!'

I laughed. 'Right... as always,' I said. 'I shall now depart to explain to Mrs Carey the rudiments of sound amortisation!'

*

In spite of her haggard appearance, I found Mrs Carey very intractable. Her mind, as I saw it, had become so set on her course of conduct that it was not easy to make an impression upon her.

'You understand, don't you, Mrs Carey,' I repeated as patiently and as kindly as I could, sitting on the wooden chair and facing her across the kitchen table, 'that your first thought must be for your husband and your little children. As far as the tombstone is concerned, it cannot possibly matter whether it is erected tomorrow or the year after next.'

I stood up, walked over to the mantelpiece, and looked at the photograph of her first husband.

'Now, Mrs Carey,' I said, 'this good-looking young man has a kind face. He would not want little children to suffer.'

I sat down again facing her. 'There is something else I want to say to you,' I went on, 'although I am a little nervous about putting it to you. I don't know whether you realise it, but if you continue to deprive your children during these important years, you may do terrible damage to them, both physically and mentally, for ever afterwards.'

Mrs Carey receive my words in silence, her eyes cast down as if she were studying the bare wooden top of the kitchen table, and I could not see her expression.

'Mrs Carey,' I tried again, 'whatever your reason may be for deciding on so very expensive a tombstone – I am sure I would appreciate your reason if I knew it – you must, at least for the sake of the children, put away only part of what you are now saving each week, and spend the rest on their happiness. That's right, isn't it?' I coaxed her.

She looked up with tears in her eyes. 'It'll only be another twelve months, if Ted keeps well,' she said.

'He won't keep well at this rate,' I answered her sharply. 'He can't continue to work on insufficient food. And what will happen when he loses his job?'

She was crying silently now. I reached across the table and put my hand on hers.

'There is a way out, you know, Mrs Carey,' I said, 'which will make everything come right. The time has now come for you and your Ted to decide to put half... no, only a quarter, away each week, and to spend the rest on better food and clothing for the family. Whatever your reason for making such terrible sacrifices, surely both your Ted and you will see the wisdom of what I am saying.'

She stood up and walked to the window, staring out without answering. I waited. Then, returning rather quickly to her seat opposite me at the table, she began to speak rapidly. There were no more tears as she spoke, but the words came from her painfully as she clasped and unclasped her thin hands.

'I don't 'ardly know 'ow to say it,' she began, 'but you won't tell nobody?'

Her tenseness made me anxious, and I suddenly felt that I didn't want to know. Before I could stop her, the broken sentences which followed exposed the torment of two souls... and it was all for so very little reason, as I was soon to learn.

'I want to tell somebody,' she faltered, 'me and Ted 'ave been carrying it all alone. You see, Joe, my first 'ubby didn't know Ted until they was in the army. Joe was a good 'usband, pretty 'andsome 'e was to look at, but there was somefin' wrong with 'im. He didn't... he couldn't...'

She paused, unable to express herself.

'He couldn't, Mrs Carey?' I said. 'You mean, normal relations between husband and wife?'

She nodded. 'Yes, that's what I mean. I tried to 'elp 'im... the doctor said I should... but 'e just couldn't. But I was 'appy with 'im, I was... and it wasn't long... and then the war broke out and Joe went to France...'

'So you were separated then.' I was helping her, I thought.

'Yes,' she said, 'my Ted and 'im was in the same platoon and they was real buddies, and when they wos talking at night Joe tells 'im about me. I know 'e didn't oughter 'ave, Joe was a good man and I think it was only because he couldn't, 'e made out to Ted that 'e was ever such a fellow...'

She looked at me. 'You know what I mean?' she asked me.

'I think I understand,' I replied.

She went on again with a rush of words. 'Joe was a good man 'e was, but 'e didn't oughter 'ave said the things 'e said to Ted... night after night they wos all alone and Joe was talkin' about me, tellin' 'im things... about me in bed, and everything...'

'Yes,' I said, 'men did strange things during the war.'

'It wasn't right,' she said simply. 'Ted knew me the way 'e didn't oughter 'ave.'

She paused and thought. 'Ted 'adn't ever seen me,' she continued, 'but 'e got a love for me and 'e wanted me; 'e couldn't think of nothink else. Then Joe got wounded terrible bad, and they sent 'im 'ome... and 'e died soon after.'

'Ted learned of his death?' I asked.

'Yes... Ted, 'e 'eard of it. 'E was 'is buddy, but 'e was glad.'

She turned her head away. 'When 'e came 'ome on leave, 'e came to see me...' She paused. 'Ted's a good man, even better'n Joe. 'E told me 'e loved me, even before 'e knew me, and 'e wanted to marry me.'

She looked at me, and then turned her head away again in shame.

'I got to love my Ted... 'e's a strong man... and I wasn't that sorry any more that Joe died...'

There was pleading in her eyes. 'You see, Ted ain't bad and I ain't that bad, but we couldn't 'elp not bein' sorry that Joe was dead... I know it's terrible, and we 'as to make it up to 'im some'ow.'

There was a long silence. I don't think she expected me to say anything. She was the first to speak again. 'You don't think Ted and me are that bad, do you ma'am?' she asked, curiously impersonal.

I put my hand on hers again. Tears trembled in her eyes and the grief on her face was pathetic.

I remained silent as thoughts followed each other through my mind – a wife who came to rejoice in the death of a loved young husband – a man exulting in the loss of an intimate friend because it gave him possession of the woman of his dreams – a tombstone as the symbol of their remorse, a sacrifice to expiate their guilt. Simple souls, cursed by conscience to the point of self-destruction.

With my hand resting lightly on hers, I told her that Joe was happy now, far happier than he would have been with her, that his marriage with her would have ended in frustration and disaster, that he could bear them no ill will for being happy and that, being a good man, what they were doing to their children would cause him sorrow if he knew it.

The tombstone, I realised, was too deep-rooted a desire to eradicate. It was only moderation which I could advise. However, when I had finished, her eyes were smiling through the tears and she agreed to talk it over with her Ted and find a compromise.

★

The twins made progress in their general condition. It was heartening to watch the school chart showing their increasing weight and height.

Before they moved up from the infant department, at the age of seven, to the junior boys, they had the usual school medical examination.

After it, I said to Mrs Carey, whose own appearance had improved, 'We are so glad the boys are doing well now.'

She smiled.

'It's been slow,' I went on, 'but with what you are doing, and with the help of the clinic, your sons are not going to be puny, are they?'

'Yes,' she agreed, 'they're coming on.'

'You're still saving for the tombstone?' I asked easily.

'Oh yes,' she answered. 'It'll only be another six months though... only six more months and it'll all be over!'

Nearly eleven years, I calculated mentally, of expiation, silently endured, in one of the most humble backstreets of London.

Even as a Hen Gathereth her Chickens...

Eight back-sloping stone steps led to the front door of Mrs Cramley's dwelling, and nine insecure stone ones were the means of access to basement level, and another door. The steps down were insecure only because the iron handrail had slipped from its moorings, and no one, least of all a member of the Cramley family, had ever thought of fixing the dangling end. It didn't seem to matter whether I risked falling backwards on the way up to the front door, or falling forwards on the way down to the basement. It was, as often as not, the door I had *not* selected for gaining admission from which Mrs Cramley would emerge. The whole house was occupied by the Cramley family and, as there were fifteen of them requiring Mrs Cramley's attention at all levels, this was not entirely a surprise.

With the hazards of entry about equal, I preferred to be admitted at basement level. The chances were that if I entered the house at the front door, I should still be obliged to descend to the basement kitchen by means of the dark, tortuous internal staircase, a somewhat dangerous journey. I would be exhorted, at each step, to 'mind the cat, the dog, or even a chicken', which might be lurking in some dark spot.

In that house, apart from twelve male children resulting from the union of Mr and Mrs Cramley, there was also one male child resulting from a mis-union of the Cramley's eldest son.

This human rabbit warren also housed a dog, a cat, two kittens, two budgerigars, an undisclosed number of chickens, a cock and a rabbit, and all the animals in the house had the same freedom of movement as the humans. I, as a friend of the family, knew that, but when the sanitary inspector called, of course, he found the hens and the cock neatly restrained behind chicken wire in the grubby backyard, and the animal life generally not quite so evident. The grapevine in that street worked perfectly.

Mrs Cramley exuded maternity. Her big, untidy body flowed out of every garment she wore. Her mane of thick brown hair escaped from even the coarse string shopping bag she often wore as a hairnet. The bouncing, bonny, grimy three-year-old baby, whose playground was the kitchen floor, was living evidence of the superfluity of germicides; the entire Cramley family must have survived every 'bug' known to medical science. Every time I entered the house, I uttered a silent prayer that the cats and the dog, at least, were better house-trained than the hens.

From the time when a benevolent government began to provide Mrs Cramley with children's allowances, she saved, largely with my help, to provide one or more of the Cramley schoolchildren with a holiday by the sea or in the country. Having calculated a sum which would be satisfactory to the charitable organisation providing the holiday home, Mrs Cramley would begin her instalment payments just after Christmas. Theoretically, there would then be enough money in my fund by the time the children went for their holiday in August.

This all worked admirably in theory. The calls of motherhood are, however, irresistibly strong. A little indulgence here or there soon broke down the theory, with the practical result that Mrs Cramley began to get behind with the payments.

It was usually then that I found myself risking life and limb to negotiate the perilous steps up to, or down to, that abode of mother love.

Mrs Cramley herself was completely unconscious of her shortcomings. I believe she would have invited the Queen herself to step right into that basement living room, where the dirt seemed as appropriate to her as cleanliness is to most other dwellings, shooing the chickens into the backyard with one hand, and beckoning her guest to enter with the other.

Nevertheless, it was apparent to everyone who entered her home that there was an intangible something which permeated that curious, malodorous household, an aura of family unity and a happiness which surmounted the dirt and the lack of worldly wealth.

When the eldest son strayed from the tightly woven bond of affection, he brought home the product of his mistake to the ever open arms of his mother, to take its rightful place among all the others, human and animal, already in residence. It was characteristic that, when the mother of her eldest son's baby did not want it, Mother Cramley opened her ample arms and gave it shelter. It was a welcome, dirty addition to that monumental chaos which was the Cramley family.

There was a welcome too, for everyone who knocked, except the sanitary inspector, whether they hammered on that front door at the top of the sloping steps, or on the basement door having made that perilous descent.

★

Early one March morning, Mrs Cramley's motherly face appeared at the slightly open door of the medical room. On her head was wedged a large, black straw hat, pronged to her abundant hair by means of two hat pins, from the ends of which hung red bobbins.

'Ken I come in?' she asked, in an agitated voice.

'Yes, do, Mrs Cramley,' I replied, as she advanced inwards and closed the door behind her. 'What's the matter?'

'Cor, Mrs Loois,' she whinnied, laying a great string bag, loaded with groceries, onto the baize-covered table and slumping down in the chair I indicated, 'it's terrible news! Wothchyer think they're a-doin' of? We're goin' to be re'oused!'

The moment, which I had feared, had come at last. The levelling hand of slum clearance was poised above the residence of Mr and Mrs Cramley and the thirteen little Cramleys.

'Now come, Mrs Cramley,' I said, 'wait until you get your breath and then tell me all about it. Doctor isn't coming in this morning and I have the room to myself.'

She was wheezing away, as much with agitation as from the effort of climbing the staircase to the medical room.

'They're goin' to re'ouse us!' she repeated dramatically, shaking her head, so that the bobbins on her hat waggled menacingly. It sounded, the way she said it, like a major catastrophe.

'Surely you're glad?' I asked.

'Glad?' She looked at me incredulously. 'Wot about me 'ends!'

'What ends?' I asked, puzzled.

'Me *ends!*' she almost shouted, 'they's layin' again!'

'Oh, the hens,' I said, with as serious expression as I could muster. 'I suppose there is the possibility that you won't be able to keep them any more?'

She wrung her hands in dismay.

'But Mrs Loois, they's layin' real well now!'

'Mrs Cramley,' I said, 'wouldn't you prefer a nice new home to those old hens?'

She looked thoroughly shocked at my suggestion, and thoroughly miserable.

'We ain't goin' in the same place neither,' she moaned.

'You and the hens?' I queried.

'Nah! Me and me ole man!' she replied. It was unusual for her to say 'me ole man'. He was always dignified by the appellation 'Mr Cramley'. She really was miserable.

'Let's get this straight, Mrs Cramley,' I said. 'You and your husband are not going to the same place?'

'Yeh!'

'And the hens?'

'They ain't goin' wiv neither of us!'

'And the children?'

'They're bein' split up, we're all bein' split up. I'm 'avin' the young 'uns. Me old man's goin' wiv the big 'uns. It ain't fair,' she grizzled, almost to herself, 'we doan wanner be split up, and me 'ends carn't go wiv me neither!'

'All this splitting up is surely only just temporary, Mrs Cramley,' I tried to console her. 'As soon as your new home is ready, you'll all be together again.'

'Not me 'ends!' she lamented once more, 'nor me dog neither... or me kittens. Oh! Mrs Loois,' she went on, as the enormity of her sorrow overwhelmed her, 'carn't yer stop 'em from splittin' us up?' Her big bosom heaved with the gigantic injustice of it.

My common sense told me it would be very much better for the children and the general hygiene of the family if the council had its way, but somehow I could not bring myself to fail her. So I reached for the telephone.

The rehousing official at the borough council offices was very much more to the point and more easily understood, but he seemed young and rather officious. The whole street of houses, including Mrs Cramley's, was due to be demolished. Because of the size of the family, it had been found necessary to divide them temporarily. As soon as the two large council flats which were being joined together for their use were ready for occupation, the Cramley family would be reunited.

The menagerie, concluded the official categorically, now resident in the Cramley household, had of course to be disposed of. They could not be permitted in the temporary homes either. The welfare of the other tenants had to be considered.

'But what about their pet dog, the kittens...' I essayed hopefully.

'No one is allowed to keep pets in the new council block in which Mrs Cramley will eventually be rehoused,' he replied.

That was obviously final and I replaced the receiver. Mrs Cramley was clasping and unclasping her hands in feverish agitation. She was searching my face anxiously for some sign of hope and I had to say something.

'The county council is mightier than the borough council and the government is mightier than the county council,' I found myself saying darkly. This wasn't very intelligent, but was a mental reaction, no doubt, to the young official.

'Have you seen the new home you're going to occupy?' I went on, endeavouring to side-track the issue.

'Yes,' she answered indifferently, 'it's like a blinkin' hoffice, it is – not like a 'ome!'

'But what about the bathroom, Mrs Cramley?' I coaxed. 'Won't it be nice to have a bathroom at last?'

She sniffed contemptuously.

'I'd rather 'ave a slipper bath in the council 'ouse,' she answered, 'I'm used to 'em. What do I want wiv a barfroom anyway! I gets a barf for 'arf price', she added, 'if I 'ave it of a mornin' wiv the council.'

The comic picture of the billowing Mrs Cramley leading the members of the borough council into a communal bath flashed before my mind's eye but, somehow, I managed to keep a straight face. Economically, she was right, of course. The cost of the fuel to her would be greater than having a bath 'with the council'.

'What about the nice new kitchen boiler?' I cajoled, 'you've got only that big battered tin thing now, and you have to heave that up on to the gas cooker.'

'Huh!' she came back at me swiftly, 'I 'as two-and-ninepennorth at the bag wash, and I boils a few 'o the w'ites meself!'

'Please Mrs Loois,' she pleaded, returning to her misfortunes and bringing every ounce of her avoirdupois to bear witness to her plight, 'we doan wanner be split up.'

'Of course you don't, Mrs Cramley,' I soothed, 'but it couldn't possibly be for long, and you will have a home which will be so much safer and so much more sanitary.'

'Ain't yer goin' to 'elp me?' she asked, aghast to find me so much less responsive than she had previously expected.

'I wish I could,' I told her, 'but what more can we do now? All the houses in the street are coming down under the clearance scheme. You have to go somewhere meanwhile, until your flat is ready for you, and you are such a large family that the borough council just can't put you all together, but it's only for a short while.'

The whimpering noises she was making distressed me. I knew what all this meant to her, and I tried to change the subject a little.

'How much will the rent of the new flat be?' I asked, hoping to get her mind away from the painful splitting-up process.

'Three times more'n wot we're payin'!' she replied, her mind elsewhere.

The older children were earning, and so was Mrs Cramley, who did some cleaning while the other children were at school. It was fortunate, no doubt, that a shortage of cleaners rendered Mrs Cramley's job fairly secure, and that her employer was unlikely ever to visit the Cramley household or to speculate upon its contents.

'That's quite a rent!' I exclaimed. 'Will you be able to pay it?'

'Oh Mrs Loois,' she whimpered again, 'I doan wanner go!'

She was rocking her ample body from side to side on the chair, completely overwhelmed by the enormity of her misery, the red bobbins on her hat swaying rhythmically as she rocked.

'What'll we do! What'll we do!' she wailed.

I just couldn't bear it. I lifted the receiver once more. The ping of the bell roused her from her abandonment to grief. She ceased moaning and watched me intently, as if the telephone on the table, adding to my importance in her estimation, and to the importance of the occasion, might save her from impending doom.

The divisional organiser was her usual helpful self but could suggest nothing, and I replaced the receiver dejectedly. Sensing my lack of success, Mrs Cramley renewed her rocking and whimpering when, fortunately, the telephone rang.

The divisional organiser was back on the line, asking whether Mrs Cramley had ever considered an application to be rehoused in one of the large older houses in the neighbourhood which the council had acquired for conversion. She added that they had the merit of being cheaper and, moreover, the authorities might more readily consent to a household pet.

I put it to Mrs Cramley. Her brows knit together in what appeared to be a real effort of concentration. Realising that it would be useless to await the outcome of her deliberations and, in order not to waste the time of the busy organiser, I made a rapid note of the particulars she gave me. While Mrs Cramley, a little more composed, was still pondering my original question, I dialled the borough housing department again. The official who answered me this time was more senior, and a good deal more understanding. He filled in the details which were missing from the organiser's information, and it seemed that there might be a chance for just one pet.

I explained it all to Mrs Cramley and repeated my question. 'Now, what about one of these larger houses?'

She thought some more.

'Wot abaht me 'ends?' she said at long last, and there just wasn't anything I could say to that.

*

The council plainly did not encourage the keeping of pets, even in the homes created by the conversion of large houses.

Mrs Cramley was, however, informed that, if her immediate neighbours raised no objection, she would be allowed to keep a cat or a dog, particularly as she had part use of the garden at the rear.

And so, at last, she had to make her heartbreaking selection. Tim, the mongrel dog, was to be saved from that 'Noah's ark'.

'Mrs Loois,' she said piteously, just before the division of the clans took place, 'will yer keep Tim ferus while we're all split up?' The inflection in her voice made the 'splitting up' sound as if a callous borough council was proposing to bisect each individual member of the family.

With a sigh which was as much out of self-pity as out of sympathetic regard for Mrs Cramley's bleak future, I consented to give the mongrel Tim a temporary refuge.

A wit once defined the neck as 'that-which-when-you-stick-it-out-you-are-up-to-in-it.' I was up to my neck in trouble. Tim's habits, engendered by his previous unrestrained life, wreaked havoc in my home.

★

The day dawned at last when, with the council's consent, Tim was to be readmitted to the bosom of his family. I knocked on the door of Mrs Cramley's new abode.

It was opened with great caution, which surprised me. However, as soon as Mrs Cramley realised it was I, bringing back one of her beloved brood, she favoured me with her broad welcoming smile.

'Cummin,' she said to me, shooing away the army of children who had followed her to the door out of curiosity.

'Be off widye,' she enjoined them, waving her stout arms in front of her, and I followed her through the hall into the kitchen, dragging Tim behind me on the lead.

The new kitchen was cleaner than the last one only because, I suspected, the Cramleys hadn't had enough time to reduce it to the 'comfort' of their former habitation. It had, nevertheless, all the stamp of the Cramley chaos.

The children fell upon their pet mongrel as soon as I unhooked the lead. Although any other dog would have been flattened by the weight of that demonstrative affection, Tim emerged triumphant from the physical onslaught upon his person, still wagging his tail.

'Happy?' I asked Mrs Cramley, smiling cheerfully.

She smiled too, and nodded. Then I noticed above her head, dangling from a hook in the ceiling, the cage with the two budgerigars.

'Yer carn't call them hanimals!' she answered my gaze.
I tried to look neutral.

'We ain't quite settled in yet,' she said, ingeniously warding off any awkward questions, 'takes a bit o' time to find the right place fer things.'

'Show me the rest of the maisonette,' I suggested.

She did so readily, sailing majestically through the kitchen door. I followed. The dog followed me, from his newly acquired habit, and the children followed the dog. Up the stairs we climbed, in that order, and, just before I reached the half-landing, Tim growled menacingly.

'Sawl right, Tim,' said one of the children behind me, 'itsony Bertha!'

There, in the darkest corner of the half-landing, was a bundle of old clothing arranged like a large bird's nest, in which Bertha, the cat, stood facing us with her back arched in anger. Slowly, perhaps recognising her former playmate Tim, she subsided again in her corner. No doubt the kittens were there too. I didn't stop to investigate. Instead, I trailed behind Mrs Cramley into one of the large bedrooms.

I duly admired the size of the room. It was not possible for me to admire the state in which she kept it, but I encouraged her to tell me that she preferred her new home to the one she had left.

Strolling over to the window, I looked down on the garden below. It was not very large, and it was certainly not enhanced by the variety of clothing hanging on the line.

We all looked out, and I thought I saw the shell of a huge tortoise on the paving stones leading to the coal bunker. The dog, the cat, the kittens, the budgerigars and now a tortoise, I counted mentally, but made no comment.

It was then that I heard unmistakable sounds, although there were no hens visible to the eye.

'Tucktheree... tuck... tuck, tucktheree... tuck... tuck... tuck!'

Without a shadow of a doubt, it was emanating from that garden below!

'Mrs Cramley,' I tried to reproach her, but my voice was shaking with suppressed laughter, 'how could you!'

The children, wise to the goings-on, sensed my mood.

'Tucktheree... tuck... tuck,' said one of the little boys, and we all rocked with laughter.

All, that is, except Mrs Cramley, who just smiled contentedly.